The Innocent Eye Test

The Innocent Eye Test

by

Michael Healey

Playwrights Canada Press
Toronto • Canada

Playwrights Canada Press
The Canadian Drama Publisher
215 Spadina Ave. Suite 230, Toronto, Ontario CANADA M5T 2C7
416.703.0013 fax 416.408.3402
orders@playwrightscanada.com • www.playwrightscanada.com

Financial support provided by the taxpayers of Canada and Ontario through the Canada Council for the Arts and the Department of Canadian Heritage through the Book Publishing Industry Development Programme, and the Ontario Arts Council.

Canada

The Canada Council for the Arts
Le Conseil des Arts du Canada

ONTARIO ARTS COUNCIL
CONSEIL DES ARTS DE L'ONTARIO

Front cover painting by Giovanni Francesco Barbieri, called Il Guercino, Italian, Emilian (1591-1666). *Saint Luke Displaying a Painting of the Virgin*, 1652-1653. Oil on canvas, 87 x 71 inches (220.98 x 180.34 cm). The Nelson-Atkins Museum of Art, Kansas City, Missouri. Purchase, F83-55. Photograph by E. G. Schempf.
Cover design: JLArt
Production Editor: MZK

Library and Archives Canada Cataloguing in Publication

Healey, Michael
The innocent eye test / Michael Healey.

A play.
ISBN 0-88754-860-1

I. Title.

PS8565.E14I56 2006 C812'.54 C2006-900645-8

First edition: March 2006.
Printed and bound by Canadian Printco at Scarborough, Canada.

Acknowledgements:

This play was initiated by David Mirvish during a very provocative phone call. Having provoked me, he and his organization then did everything they could to help.

I owe special thanks to Linda Intaschi and Kelly Robinson for their support and notes during the play's development. I am grateful to the artist Mark Tansey for his positive reaction to my script, and I count as one of the chief pleasures of this project the opportunity to contact and pester someone whose work I've admired for a decade.

My thanks to the actors who have read the play's various drafts to me. And my gratitude and affection to Christopher Newton, whose sense of humour (and of the theatrical) has challenged me throughout the process.

The Innocent Eye Test premiered February 9, 2006 at the Manitoba Theatre Centre in coproduction with Mirvish Productions, with the following company:

SAMUEL Kneck . . . . .Kevin Bundy
COLLEEN MacAuley . . . . .Tanja Jacobs
MOUI Lamaz .Lisa Norton
URI . . . . .Gordon Rand
JAMES MacAuley . . . . .C. David Johnson
DARRYL Plate . . . . .Tom McCamus
MARTINO Kesselback . . . . .Keith James
Directed by Christopher Newton

Set Design: David Beochler
Lights Design: Kevin Lamotte
Stage Manager: Laurie Champagne

Setting: An immense Tuscan villa, recently transformed into an expensive resort and spa.

ACT ONE

Scene One

The first act takes place poolside at the villa. Many chaises, many fluffy towels. Umbrellas provide shade from the relentless Tuscan sun. The shallow end of the pool is downstage left; the rest of the pool runs off left. In the dark, we hear someone speaking in voice-over. The lights first come up on SAMUEL, seated on a chaise, in a full suit of clothes. He holds a briefcase to his chest. We hear his thoughts:

SAMUEL (*voiceover*) …I don't know. Can you sue Air Canada? Can a person sue Air Canada for the food that they shovel at?— Probably not. Probably immune from prosecution like the President of the— Ten-hour flight, I feel like I'm eighty years old. Kill for something to eat. The bun, good God, I dropped the Air Canada bun on my foot and nearly broke my— How could the room not be ready? What is it, like five o'clock? (*checks his watch*) In Toronto it's—so here it must be—I don't know. When am I supposed to meet the guy? When did the thing say? Where did I leave the thing? In my bag. (*looks around*) Aw, jeez, where's the bag. Oh, yeah, bag's okay. Tuscan bellhop has it. Relax, Sam. I hope he doesn't dump it into a ditch.… He looked like he was going to wipe his nose with the tip I— Better not lose this. (*clutches the briefcase closer*) Guy must be nuts. Sends me cash. We didn't even talk money. Another one of these nuts, these art-loving, rich nuts with money to— Nice out here. Italy. Nice and hot. I could sleep. Sammy, you can't go to sleep. You got this guy's money.

Lights have by now come up. MOUI Lamaz is revealed, seated in another chaise. Dressed for the sun. She glances at SAMUEL.

(*voiceover*) Did she?— Wow. She looked at me. She totally and absolutely looked at me, I think. Yeah, right, Sammy, why would she be looking at you? Just relax. The money's making you paranoid. First thing I'm gonna do when I see this guy is hand him his money back. Then we'll talk. What kind of a guy buys a painting for cash? No, what kind of a guy, deciding to buy a painting, sends a huge load of cash that gets to the hotel where he's supposed to meet the guy selling the painting, and it gets there on its own before he does? Well, whatever. I'm just happy to make the sale. It's been months since—

MOUI rises, crosses past SAMUEL to retrieve a towel.

(*voiceover*) Hooo-eee. She's, she's… incredible. Are all the women in Tuscany incredible? Wow. And, I mean, come on, those legs, they go all the way up. Ha ha ha—oh, Sammy. Funny guy. I'm a funny—for Christ's sake, Sam, stop staring. (*He looks away.*) Jeez. Ha ha. Pervert. She's waay outta your league, Sammy boy. It's the heat. Plus, has anyone actually ever slept on one of those godawful Air Canada—

MOUI (*as she passes, in a not-very-good Australian accent*) Good morning.

SAMUEL Good morning. Morning.

MOUI returns to her seat, tucking the towel under her head.

(*voiceover*) Okay. All right. I think she likes me…. Good morning? It's morning? Wait a minute. (*looks at his watch again*) It's got to be afternoon, right? It's the morning in Toronto, ten-hour flight, time difference between here and there is…

MOUI (*sitting up*) Sorry. I mean: good afternoon.

SAMUEL Oh. Right. Ha ha. Good afternoon.

MOUI Ha ha. Sorry, um, mate.

SAMUEL No, please. My mistake.

She smiles at him. A moment, then she reclines.

(*voiceover*) All right Sammy. In Italy for 15 minutes and already the magic is working. Sammy boy. This is, you know what? I'm going to enjoy this. This trip. Get the thing done with the guy, sell the painting, then take all this cash and have myself some fun. Stay here for six months, screw the business, stop fighting it, let it fall apart; take all this money, and lavish it on someone like her, and, and have fun. Be that guy, that guy who… has fun, goddam it. Be that guy. For once. With that girl. That amazing girl right over—you are the most beautiful—you are, you are just—(*singing*) Rooooxanne. You don't have to put on the red light. Roooooooooooooxanne. (*MOUI smiles to herself.*) You don't have to wear that dress tonight. (*MOUI laughs to herself.*) Roooooox—God, I could use a drink. I'm soaking through this suit. Not even paid for yet, and I'm soaking through—I don't know why you bought it. You can't afford it. I hope this guy is paying for all this, God knows I can't. In fact, if I don't make this sale, then I'm completely— Love a bottle of water. Something. Or a beer. Oh, God, LOVE a beer. Ha ha. One beer and I'd slide off the side of this mountain. Great. Love a beer though. How do you—what's the Italian for beer, I wonder?

MOUI *Birra.*

A beat.

SAMUEL Sorry?

MOUI Beer in Italian. Is *birra.* Mate. It says so, right here. In my Australian-Italian phrase book.

SAMUEL It's?…

MOUI Oh.

SAMUEL What?—

MOUI (*The Australian accent unravels a bit. Underneath it is an American accent.*) You didn't, that wasn't—

SAMUEL How?— I—

MOUI That wasn't out loud, was it. Oh, jeez.

She rises, gathers her things.

SAMUEL Sorry, did I speak?

MOUI No, you didn't. You didn't say anything. Jeez. I knew I'd be no good at this. Sorry, mister. Mate.

MOUI leaves.

SAMUEL Wait! How did you know I—

But she's gone. After some time he looks around, and, seeing no one, opens the briefcase.

Jesus.

He begins to pull out wads of different kinds of cash, setting them on the chaise before him.

Must be ten different kinds of cash in here. Rupees… Euros… what are those, New Zealand dollars? Prindars… what are prindars? My God. The guy's nuts.

He hears a splash at the other end of the pool. He quickly replaces all the cash in the briefcase. He sits. COLLEEN MacAuley swims to the shallow end of the pool, and pulls herself out. She looks around for a towel. She looks at SAMUEL, who smiles politely. She looks at the towel that's within his reach. He cottons, grabs the towel and, rising, offers it to her. She takes it. As she does so:

COLLEEN Are you my guy?

SAMUEL Sorry?

COLLEEN Sorry. I screwed it up. Let me start again. Colostomy?

SAMUEL I beg your pardon?

COLLEEN Colostomy. Colostomy.

SAMUEL What?

COLLEEN Colostomy? (*nodding to his briefcase*) Colostomy bag?

SAMUEL What? No. That's—

COLLEEN Are you my guy?

SAMUEL Your guy?

COLLEEN You're dressed like my guy. They said— Shit. What am I doing wrong here. Colostomy.

SAMUEL I don't know what you're saying to me. I don't speak, *nona parlo—*

COLLEEN Sorry. Are you Uri?

SAMUEL Am I what?

COLLEEN Uri? Are you here for the buy?

SAMUEL The?… Oh, yes, the buy.

COLLEEN Okay. Good. (*the briefcase*) Is that it?

SAMUEL It's— Are you Mr. Plate?

COLLEEN Am I what?

SAMUEL I was expecting a Mr. Plate?

COLLEEN Is that code? Plate? (*Suddenly, she sees someone at the other end of the pool.*) Oh! James! Hello! Come here! (*sotto voce, to SAMUEL*) Good going.

The sound of someone diving into the deep end of the pool.

(*to SAMUEL*) Okay, just be cool, and we'll do it later. Way to go. Okay. Sorry.

SAMUEL What are we doing?

COLLEEN Sorry about this. I don't really know what I'm doing here.

SAMUEL You don't?

COLLEEN No. It's but it's okay. We'll do it. Don't worry.

SAMUEL Um.

COLLEEN We'll do it in a little while. Don't worry. Say something.

SAMUEL Uh…

COLLEEN It's okay, it's my husband. Say something.

SAMUEL Uh, isn't it, uh, nice. The… uh…

COLLEEN (*loudly and conversationally*) Which?

SAMUEL That's a nice… pool.

COLLEEN Which pool? Oh, the pool! That pool! Yes! Italian!

COLLEEN dissolves in laughter. JAMES swims up, pulls himself from the pool.

JAMES Bothering the other guests, my dear?

COLLEEN That's right, darling. You know me.

JAMES Do I ever. She'll talk to anyone. Hello.

SAMUEL Ha ha.

COLLEEN Darling, this is, um…

SAMUEL Samuel Kneck.

JAMES James MacAuley. How do you do?

COLLEEN I saw him first.

JAMES Okay.

SAMUEL Sorry?

JAMES Ha ha.

COLLEEN Ha ha. I mean it.

JAMES Okay, okay. (*to SAMUEL*) Lovely spot, eh?

SAMUEL It's, yes. It's beautiful.

JAMES American, are you?

SAMUEL Yes. No. Not really. Canadian. Sorry.

JAMES Ah. I presume you know my auntie in Vancouver?

SAMUEL Oh, well, I don't know. Where does she, what's her—

COLLEEN Stop teasing the man, for God's sake Jimmy.

JAMES Yes. Sorry. Three years of marriage have made me a compulsive bully, I'm afraid.

SAMUEL Oh. Well. Ha ha.

COLLEEN Me too!

All laugh. COLLEEN smacks SAMUEL playfully. More laughter. A pause.

JAMES Funny swim togs.

SAMUEL Oh. Ha ha. My room isn't ready yet. I haven't had a chance to change.

JAMES Staying long?

SAMUEL A few days, I think.

JAMES Terrific. Maybe you'd join us for dinner one night? And then, after dinner, who knows? We can do what ever it is consenting adults get up to here in Tuscany.

SAMUEL Well, that sounds—

COLLEEN Now look, darling, I'm not telling you again. He's mine.

JAMES Yes, darling, I know. He's not really my type, anyhow. I was only suggesting an innocent game of cards or something. Poker?

SAMUEL Sorry? Well, she asked for a towel, so I—

JAMES Do you play? Do they play poker in Canada?

COLLEEN No, they don't.

SAMUEL Well, they, yes, but—

JAMES I've put a little game together for tonight. Me and some of the other desperately bored husbands.

SAMUEL Oh, uhh. I'm not, I have to meet someone.

JAMES Don't we all.

COLLEEN Not all of us. Some of us are just here for a holiday. (*to SAMUEL, suggestively*) Isn't that right?

SAMUEL Well, actually, I'm here to do a little business—

COLLEEN No you're not!

She smacks SAMUEL, then kisses him.

Isn't he adorable!

JAMES He certainly is. We'll talk again once you're settled. Come along, dear. I'm dying for a drink.

COLLEEN Of course you are.

JAMES jumps into the pool, swims away.

(*whispers*) Stay. Here. Colostomy.

COLLEEN makes a few vague gestures to SAMUEL, and then follows JAMES. SAMUEL is left alone again. He finally decides to leave the patio, in the hope that his room is ready. As he strides off, a man enters, directly in his path. The man, gaunt and weedy, wears a shabby dark suit and clutches a briefcase to his chest. He and SAMUEL stop. A pause. Finally:

URI Colostomy?

SAMUEL Uhh…

URI Do you… colostomy?

SAMUEL Well, no, I… sell art.

URI Sell art?

SAMUEL Yes.

URI Irish?

SAMUEL Canadian.

URI No freaking good. (*motions for SAMUEL to leave*) Get out of it.

SAMUEL I was just going—

URI Out of pool, Canadian. Beat the road.

SAMUEL No, sure.

He goes.

URI Hey, Canada.

SAMUEL stops.

Canada sucks.

SAMUEL I'm sorry?

URI Canada is shit country.

SAMUEL Well, I— What do you mean?

URI Canada is to USA as my grandma is to Pamela Anderson. Ha ha.

SAMUEL Okay.

URI Canada is to USA like a pile of dog fecee is beside majestic Matterhorn. You know Yugo? The car?

SAMUEL Uhh…

URI Canada is the Yugo, and USA is the Cadillac. Know what I mean? Canada sucks, Canada.

SAMUEL You know—

URI Out of pool.

SAMUEL goes. URI looks around, sets the briefcase down on a chaise, and carefully unshackles himself from it. He looks at the pool, goes to it, kneels and puts a hand in. Both hands. He splashes water on his face. He might weep. He plunges his head into the pool, and just as he does, COLLEEN rushes in.

COLLEEN Okay. I don't have much time. Let's get this done.

She heads for the briefcase and picks it up. URI emerges from the water in time to see her.

URI Hey! What you—

The briefcase explodes white powder, covering COLLEEN. It also makes a noise: Bing Crosby singing "White Christmas", mixed with a car alarm. URI grabs the briefcase from her. He shuts the noise off.

COLLEEN Oh dear God!

URI Don't touch my stuff. What you doing, crazy batch?

COLLEEN I'm sorry. Was there a man here, about your height, wearing a suit— Jesus Christ. What's that smell?

URI That's the powdered rotten egg powder I put in there to keep people like you out of my stuff. Now you stink.

COLLEEN I'm sorry. I didn't mean to— What happened to the other man? I have orders. I have to make contact with the other man.

URI That was just Canada. He leave.

COLLEEN All right. I'm sorry—

URI Learn this lesson: don't touch the stuff of another.

COLLEEN No. Okay. I—

COLLEEN begins to weep, and goes. URI puts the briefcase down, under a chaise. He returns to the water, and removing his socks and shoes, plunges his feet in. He rolls up his pants to put his legs in, and pulls out his shirt. It's too much. He can't bear the feeling, and begins to remove his jacket, shirt and pants. He's in a frenzy now, and, slowed by a button or belt, he throws himself into the pool. After a long time under, he surfaces.

URI Ohhhh God. Ohhhh.

Calmer now, he removes his remaining clothing. As he pulls off his underpants, putting them on the deck, he looks toward the villa.

CAN I GET BEER?

He smacks his head repeatedly to dislodge some water from his ear.

Blackout.

Scene Two

Early evening. Soft, twinkling lights, and light from inside the pool. SAMUEL, now dressed more appropriately but still clutching the briefcase, walks with DARRYL Plate.

DARRYL Canada. You know what Canada's problem is?

SAMUEL Well, yes, actually, I do.

DARRYL You do? Oh. Well. Good for you. What was I saying?

SAMUEL I don't, um—

DARRYL Oh, yeah: people. What do people want. The trickiest thing about assessing what the people want is that they'll tell you they want one thing, and then their actions will show they want something else entirely. Sometimes the thing they want is the actual complete opposite of the thing they said they wanted. So it's a struggle. It's fun, though, too, right? Like for instance: there are like 30 million people who get off planes in Vegas every year. Average age of these people is, I dunno, like 92. And about a third of them stay an average of three and a half nights in one of the half-dozen properties I own.

SAMUEL Oh, so, that's what you do?

DARRYL Sorry?

SAMUEL You own casinos? In Las Vegas?

DARRYL takes SAMUEL's arm and they stop. DARRYL regards SAMUEL for a moment.

DARRYL You're kidding me. You have no idea who I am.

SAMUEL I'm sorry, Mr. Plate, uh—

DARRYL Darryl.

SAMUEL —Darryl. I just don't travel in those circles, and—

DARRYL Fantastic. I love it. But why would you come all this way to sell me a painting if you have no idea who I am?

SAMUEL Well, um, you asked.

DARRYL I see.

SAMUEL You sent me a plane ticket.

DARRYL You came because I asked. I love it. Canada. Yes. I own some hotels. One of them is called the Tuscany, and it looks exactly like this place, only classier. What was I saying?

SAMUEL You were going to tell me what people want.

DARRYL Right. I got a dozen guys who work for me, and their job is to sweat blood if occupancy in any of my hotels drops below 95%. So they come to me one day and say: we did a survey, and we are 100% convinced that people who come to Las Vegas want more shows. They want Broadway—no more with the topless girls lip-syncing to the Bee Gees, they want the real thing. Big Broadway musical. Give them that and you can bury the competition. So I go: great. And I head off in search of a show to bring in. That was fun. I go to New York, I start seeing show after show, I meet—did you ever meet Chita Rivera?

SAMUEL No, I didn't.

DARRYL Oh, please. I mean, shut up. Fantastic lady. Absolutely beautiful, and tough as hell, and just all around my kind of gal. And she's doing *Chicago*. You know this show?

SAMUEL Yes.

DARRYL Really?

SAMUEL No, not really.

DARRYL The perfect show for Vegas. It's about bad people winning, it's sexy, it stars the unforgettable Chita Rivera. So we bring it out, we put it on. First half goes great. Old guys standing on the tables, applauding, whistling. A half-dozen respirators break down. Second half starts, place goes quiet. And stays that way. Chita, she can't understand it. Then she hears this noise, like chink chink, chink chink. And it gets louder, and louder, this noise. Chink chink, CHINK CHINK. Know what it is?

SAMUEL Uh, no—

DARRYL It's half the audience, getting up in the middle of the show, they've all got a bucket of quarters for the slots, which they now absolutely must get back to. Lights come up at the end, Chita comes out for her, you know, her bow, and there are 60 people left. Ms Chita Rivera is not pleased, needless to say. So, I let her out of the contract, and I fire the dozen guys who begged me to bring Broadway to the desert. You want a beer?

SAMUEL Uh, sure.

DARRYL *(looking back toward the villa) Dos cervecas por favor.*

SAMUEL Um…

DARRYL And then I do what I wanted to do in the first place, which is I built a pond. Right in front of the Tuscany. I put a fountain in the middle of the pond, I play the "William Tell Overture" thirty times a day and the fountain water squirts in time to the music. It lasts three and a half minutes. Huge round of applause at the end. Never fails. Then they go back to handing over their retirement fund to my blackjack dealers.

SAMUEL Wow.

DARRYL I know. And do you think if I asked those people if they wanted to see the dancing waters of my magnificent fountain, they'd say they definitely would want to see that? Of course not. They want Broadway shows. People don't know what they want. That's the problem with the world. Nobody knows what they want, but woe betide anyone who points that out. People who tell people that get burned at the stake. Throughout like history.

There is a thoughtful pause.

SAMUEL Mr. Plate?

DARRYL Darryl?

SAMUEL Darryl?

DARRYL Samuel?

SAMUEL So, about this painting…

DARRYL No.

SAMUEL No?

DARRYL Not yet. We haven't established a, like a thing, yet, a whaddayacall…

SAMUEL A rapport?

DARRYL Yeah.

SAMUEL Oh. Okay.

DARRYL (*of the briefcase*) Let's have a look.

SAMUEL Yes. Thank you.

SAMUEL eagerly hands over the briefcase. DARRYL opens it up and dumps all the money onto a chair. He sorts it and puts it back into the briefcase during the following.

DARRYL I love cash. We take in something like a half-billion dollars in coins and bills in a year. Sometimes I just go into the counting rooms, stand there as they pile it up and up. Never understood the appeal of the bank draft, the cashier's cheque, the wire transfer. Wire transfer? Digits on a computer screen. Who cares? Gimme the cash. You know how much is there?

SAMUEL No. A lot?

DARRYL You bet. There's about 180,000 US dollars right there. Whenever I can, I like to do business in cash. Makes it more real, somehow.

URI enters, his briefcase under an arm, noisily eating an entire roast chicken without the aid or impediment of utensils. He clocks the pile of money on the way by, gives the two men a look. He sits off to himself, dropping the spent bits of carcass on the pool deck.

SAMUEL Is this all from your casinos?

DARRYL Oh, yeah. People bring all this money from all over the world, leave it with me. Look at that. Prindars! You know, if every casino in Vegas turned over their profits from a single year to the government, education in America would be fixed for an entire generation.

SAMUEL Really?

DARRYL Yeah. Not that that'll happen, but it's a nice thought.

SAMUEL Yes, I guess it is.

DARRYL Are you charmed yet?

SAMUEL I'm sorry?

DARRYL Am I charming you yet?

SAMUEL Well, uh, Darryl. You seem… nice.

DARRYL Sammy, I been called a lotta things, but nice…

SAMUEL And, but, why do I need to be charmed, Darryl?

DARRYL Several reasons. First, to see if it can be done. I mean, I know what I'm like, and I'm beginning to get a feel for what you're like, and I know that your kind of intelligent, sensitive, Canadian type of person is generally put off by the likes of me.

SAMUEL Oh, no.

A beat.

DARRYL That's all the protest you can muster?

SAMUEL Well—

DARRYL Never mind. We both know I'm right. It's okay. I'm used to it. The whole of Europe is put off by the likes of me. Including Canada. It's okay. The other reason I'm trying to charm you is because if I don't there's no way in hell you're going to sell me that painting.

SAMUEL What makes you say that?

DARRYL Well, Sam, I don't think you're going to approve of what I want to do with it.

SAMUEL What are you going to do with it?

DARRYL I'm going to put it in a gallery and charge people ten bucks to look at it.

SAMUEL Well, uh, that sounds—

DARRYL Sounds okay when I put it like that, doesn't it? But that's not the thing here. Look. I've decided to open a gallery in the Tuscany. I have this feeling that people will appreciate a little culture to go with their debauchery. They get to go home and say "I saw art" and leave out the fact they dropped the dialysis money playing craps. But you and I know that nothing makes you sleepier faster than walking into a friggin' museum. And I don't want 'em sleepy. I pump pure oxygen into the casino to keep 'em awake.

URI drops the chicken, heads back inside.

Jeez. How about that guy.

SAMUEL I know. He screamed at me earlier.

DARRYL What for?

SAMUEL I have no idea. He wanted me to leave the pool.

DARRYL And what did you do?

SAMUEL I, well, I left.

DARRYL Uh huh.

After a beat.

Where was I?

SAMUEL The gallery?

DARRYL The gallery. It's going to be great. I got everything, all the greatest hits. I got a da Vinci, I got a Picasso, I got a Veer Meer, I got a Manet or a Monet, or maybe one of each, I don't remember. I got a big-ass Warhol. I got sculpture, I got tapestries, I got little pencil sketches from Dutch dudes. I been all over Europe, the last couple of months, buying this stuff up.

SAMUEL Sounds like a large collection.

DARRYL It's gonna be big. I've spent maybe 200 million dollars so far. That doesn't include the gallery itself.

It's gonna be fantastic. The whole place is geared to keeping you awake and moving. We're gonna have music, 24/7, and nice bright lights, and—and here's the best part—the floor's gonna move.

SAMUEL Really?

DARRYL Yup. You just step on, and the floor whizzes you past the whole collection. Never stops. You see the whole thing—I got Don Rickles to tell you about every picture by sticking a thing in your ear—and 10 minutes later you get deposited in the gift shop.

SAMUEL Well, that sounds—

DARRYL Disgusting, right?

SAMUEL Yeah. Kind of.

DARRYL There you go. If I'm you, I'd hate the idea. Old people in sweat suits standing on a conveyor belt, blowing past millions of dollars in art. It's kind of a disgusting mental image. So it's going to take all this money plus all my charm to get you to sell me the picture. You like it a lot, am I right?

SAMUEL Well, yes, but—

DARRYL Sure. It's probably a very nice picture. Who made it again?

SAMUEL Mark Tansey.

DARRYL Oh yeah, that's right. Is it a nice painting?

SAMUEL You don't know?

DARRYL No. I mean, I assume it's nice.

SAMUEL You have no idea what painting it is you're here to buy?

DARRYL Well, I wouldn't say I have no idea. I don't know what it looks like and I don't know who made it, but apart from that, I'm very focused.

URI comes back with a bottle of wine, open, no glass, and an entire cake. As he passes the men:

URI Good food here, what? Boys?

SAMUEL Uh, yes.

DARRYL The best.

URI (*sitting down*) Ohhh, crep, yeah.

URI begins eating and drinking.

DARRYL I hope he hangs around. Next to him, I come off like the Duke of friggin' Windsor.

They watch URI for a few beats.

SAMUEL What were you saying?

DARRYL Hmm? Oh. The painting. What's it called?

SAMUEL The "Innocent Eye Test".

DARRYL That's right. It's a big one, am I right?

SAMUEL It's important. Maybe not as important as some of the other paintings you've acquired, but—

DARRYL No, I mean, it takes up space, am I right?

SAMUEL Well, yes, it's about ten feet wide and six feet high.

DARRYL Right. Well, here it is: They're building the gallery, it's going up fast, and my guy comes to me and he says: "They built an extra wall." I don't know how it happened, but there's an extra chunk of space I have to use up in the contemporary American section. So my art guy suggests this "Innocent" whatever. It's like exactly the same size as this new wall they put in. Isn't that great?

SAMUEL Uh…

DARRYL Plus, it matches the carpet. It's mostly beige, right? This picture?

SAMUEL Well, yes. It's monochromatic.

DARRYL Monochromatically beige, yeah?

SAMUEL Yes.

DARRYL So. There you go. It's perfect for my needs. What do you say?

SAMUEL Well, Darryl—

DARRYL You're disgusted. I've disgusted you.

SAMUEL No no, not at all. What a buyer does with something after I—

DARRYL No, you're disgusted. That's okay. I like a challenge. Look. You're a straight man, right?

SAMUEL Sorry?

DARRYL Sexually? Sorry, it's just, it's sometimes hard to tell with you people.

SAMUEL Yes I am.

DARRYL Right. Stay here.

DARRYL gets up and leaves. SAMUEL waits. URI rises, belches, and starts to remove his clothing languorously.

URI Hey. Canada.

SAMUEL Yes?

URI Nice night.

SAMUEL Yes. What are you doing?

URI I'm eating, I'm drinking, I'm swimming. I'm being by the pool. I have meeting. What are you doing?

SAMUEL I'm trying to sell that guy a—

URI is down to his underpants.

—Oh jeez.

URI What you selling?

SAMUEL (*averting his gaze*) A painting.

URI To that guy? He's got no taste. I could tell that from over there. The Americans are great, but they got no taste for art. Or don't you got a conscience about that sorta thing? About who gets your art?

URI is inserting earplugs.

SAMUEL Well, I—

URI ANYWAY. WATCH MY STUFF, OKAY? BUT DON'T TOUCH MY THING. MY… (*he mimes briefcase*) DON'T LEAVE POOL.

URI puts on some goggles and slips into the water. MOUI enters, hesitates, then walks over to SAMUEL.

MOUI (*The Australian accent has reinstated itself.*) Good evening. May I?

SAMUEL Oh. Hello. Of course.

She sits. There is a pause.

(*voiceover*) Say something.

(*out loud*) Nice night.

MOUI Yes, it is. It's a ripper, as we say.

A pause.

SAMUEL (*voiceover*) Very good, you idiot. Say something else.

(*out loud*) I'm Sam. Samuel Kneck.

(*voiceover*) You smell fantastic.

MOUI I'm—

URI WHAT YOU SAY?

SAMUEL Nothing. I'm not—

URI WHAT?

SAMUEL —I'm not talking to you.

URI I CAN'T HEAR. YOU TALKING TO LADY?

SAMUEL Yes.

URI OH. GOOD LUCK. SHE OUT OF YOUR LEAGUE, BUDDY. WATCH THE STUFF. DON'T TOUCH THE STUFF.

URI swims off left. During the following, we can hear him whooping and diving offstage.

MOUI Do you know him?

SAMUEL Not really. He yelled at me earlier. I'm Sam.

(*voiceover*) You said that.

MOUI Yes. It's okay. I'm Moui.

SAMUEL Moui. Hi.

They shake hands.

MOUI Moui Lamaz.

SAMUEL Sam Kneck.

(*voiceover*) Great. Shut up, already.

(*out loud*) I can't seem to stop telling you my name.

MOUI It's okay. You must be sleepy. You travelled today, right?

SAMUEL That's right.

MOUI I got here yesterday. From Australia. I'm Australian. I've been divorced for six months. What do you do in Canada?

A beat.

SAMUEL That's right, I am from Canada. Is it that obvious?

MOUI Oh, shit.

SAMUEL How did you know?

MOUI No, I didn't. Sorry. Where are you from, Sam?

SAMUEL Well, Ms Lamaz, I'm from Canada. Where are you from?

MOUI Las Vegas. I mean, Auckland.

SAMUEL Do you know a Darryl Plate?

MOUI I like to surf. Do you like to surf?

SAMUEL You're part of Darryl Plate's sales job?

MOUI (*reaching for his chest*) You have really ripper pecs, mate.

SAMUEL Please stop.

(*voiceover*) I knew it was to good too be true. No way she'd have anything to do with me.

MOUI (*The Australian accent falls away.*) That's not true. You seem very nice.

SAMUEL Sorry?

MOUI Um. Nothing.

SAMUEL I'm a little disappointed in your boss.

MOUI Don't be. He asked me to get to know you a little, that's all.

SAMUEL I see.

(*voiceover*) What the hell is that supposed to mean?

(*out loud*) Meaning what.

MOUI I'm not a hooker, if that's what you're asking. I'm a performer. I'm in a show at the Galapagos Resort and Casino.

SAMUEL (*voiceover*) Nice going. You called her a hooker. Say "I'm sorry."

(*out loud*) I'm sorry.

MOUI (*simultaneous with his spoken "I'm sorry"*) It's okay. I don't blame you. I know how this looks. And we were trying to trick you. We had a whole story. I was supposed to be an Australian divorcee on vacation alone in Italy. And we'd meet, and I'd just start talking to you.

SAMUEL I see.

MOUI But there was supposed to be no, you know, none of that. Just meet you, talk to you, find out what you're like. Mr. Plate will do anything to find out something about someone he wants something from. Anyway. Sorry.

SAMUEL It's okay.

MOUI Thanks. I told him I'd be no good at this kind of thing. I have a hard enough time keeping my real story straight. Can I just sit here for a minute?

SAMUEL Sure. Stay as long as you like.

MOUI Thanks.

SAMUEL (*voiceover*) Stay all night. Beautiful night. Let's just stay out here and just stay here.

(*out loud*) So what's the act?

MOUI Hmm? Oh. I'm a psychic's assistant. Have you ever heard of Martino Kesselback?

SAMUEL No.

MOUI Lucky you. He's a pig. You should see what goes on in his head.

SAMUEL Is he famous? Should I know him?

MOUI He's famous in the clairvoyancy trade.

SAMUEL I see.

MOUI As a pig.

SAMUEL I see.

MOUI I hired him, but he's the headline. He's onstage blindfolded while I'm in the audience holding somebody's watch. He goes "It's a watch, it's gold, a Rolex, given to him by his wife named Peggy who has six toes and a father named Seymour." Applause applause. For him. For the great Kesselback.

SAMUEL And, so, how does he do it?

MOUI He doesn't do it. That's the point. He's a fraud. I do it. I'm the clairvoyant. I do all the work, I gather all the information, and then I have to go into his head and give it to him.

SAMUEL You have to, sorry?

MOUI But while I'm in there he has the most disgusting thoughts. On purpose. You wouldn't believe some of the things. I've asked him to stop. He won't do it. It's a form of harassment. I filed a grievance with the Nevada Human Rights Commission, but nothing happened. You don't believe me, it's okay. Nobody ever does. Anyway, in exchange for my help here, Mr. Plate is going to help me get rid of the guy and find a new partner.

SAMUEL Really.

MOUI And as long as I'm being completely honest, you should know that Mr. Plate wanted me to spend some time in there (*points to SAMUEL's head*) and then report back.

SAMUEL Really.

MOUI Yeah. Like most really successful people, he's deeply insecure. He doesn't think he can convince you on his own to sell him the painting.

SAMUEL Why does he want it so badly? He doesn't even know what it looks like.

MOUI Oh, he doesn't really care. Mr. Plate likes to think of himself as the greatest negotiator on the planet. He's happiest when he's talking somebody into or out of something, it doesn't matter what. And he'll use whatever will work. That's why he tried to ruin you.

SAMUEL He what?

MOUI That's why he—oh, jeez. You don't know about that either, do you? God, I'm bad at this.

SAMUEL What do you mean? What did he do?

MOUI Well, he bought the building your gallery is in, and then he tripled your rent.

SAMUEL He bought the building?

MOUI And he sort of messed around with your credit rating, too. I don't know the details. But you're pretty hard up at the moment, right?

SAMUEL Well, yes, actually.

MOUI He's just trying to make you more receptive to the deal.

SAMUEL I see. Can you tell what I'm thinking right now?

MOUI Yes, but you're not thinking anything, are you?

SAMUEL I… no, I guess not. Just a sec.

MOUI Take your time.

SAMUEL Uuum:

(*voiceover*) Can you hear me, Ms Lamaz?

MOUI Call me Moui.

SAMUEL Thank you, Moui, call me Sa— Wow! That's!— How about now?

(*voiceover*) Darryl Plate didn't have to go to all this trouble to get the painting. He didn't need to involve you. But I'm glad he did.

MOUI Me too.

SAMUEL (*out loud*) Wow! Really? Um, wow.

A pause.

MOUI Roooxanne…

SAMUEL Hmm? Oh. Ha ha. Oh. Ew. I didn't—

URI has floated back into view.

URI HEY! CANADA! ANYBODY COME?

MOUI I better go.

SAMUEL Don't go.

MOUI No, I better. You seem nice. You guys don't need me. I guess I'll have to find some other way to fix up my act.

SAMUEL (*voiceover, the sound fading as she exits*) Come back. Come back, Moui Lamaz. If you can really read my mind, stop and turn around. I want to know if you can really hear my…

URI ANYBODY HERE?

SAMUEL What? No.

URI HEY?

SAMUEL No! You ignorant…

URI gets out of the pool. He sits near SAMUEL.

URI Good, good. That's good. Nice, hey? You been here before?

SAMUEL No.

URI The outdoors here is nicer than the ones at home.

SAMUEL Uh huh.

URI Air is softer, water is softer, moon is fetter. Look. Look at moon.

SAMUEL It's what?

URI Fetter.

SAMUEL Feta?

URI Not literally fetter, but fetter as in poetry. Look.

SAMUEL Yes.

URI Where I come from, it's hard air, hard water, dirt is harder, rocks, forget it. And moon is skinny. I see why people pay all the money they have to visit here.

SAMUEL Look—

URI I see why people get money any how to come here. I would probably kill a guy to come here, if I knew this place was here. Probably my whole country would kill a guy to get to this place. Good thing a place like this is, nobody tells about it. My whole country finds out, it's killing and then coming.

SAMUEL What's your country?

URI Ukraine.

SAMUEL Ah.

A beat.

URI That's it? That's all you got to say about Ukraine? After all I said about Canada?

SAMUEL I guess.

URI That's exactly what I mean about you. Ukraine is ass-end of globe, and you don't say nothing. Where's the girl?

SAMUEL She went back inside.

URI She was total hot. Friend of yours?

SAMUEL No.

URI But she could, if you tried. You have to try, Canada.

SAMUEL Okay, thanks.

URI Even I know that. And look where I come from.

SAMUEL Yes, okay. Can we just, do you mind?

URI Okay.

A pause.

The air is so sweet. It's beyond my thoughts.

A pause.

Hey. You mind if I fart?

SAMUEL What? Look—

URI I'm thinking of creating fart in near future. You mind?

SAMUEL Please. Leave me alone. I just want to—

URI Do you mind if I fart?

SAMUEL I don't want to, could you just—

URI DO YOU MIND IF I FART?

SAMUEL I don't care. Leave me alone.

URI OF COURSE YOU DO. Of course you mind.

SAMUEL Okay, okay—

URI You got to say. You got to say it.

SAMUEL Leave me alone, okay?

URI That's how you get girl. You got to say. I know you five minutes, Canada, I know exactly what your problem is.

SAMUEL Don't, just, don't talk to me, anymore, okay?

URI Don't talk?

SAMUEL Yes. Please.

URI Okay.

URI gets up to go.

You sure? Is nice night, and I think we having fun. Or are you sick about girl?

SAMUEL Please. Shut up. Please.

URI Oh. Okay. Shut up please.

URI crosses to his things. DARRYL charges on.

DARRYL Hey.

URI Don't talk to him. Doesn't want to hear it, him.

SAMUEL Darryl, look—

DARRYL "A painted picture is a vehicle. You can sit in your driveway and take it apart or you can get in it and go somewhere."

SAMUEL Uh huh.

DARRYL That's your guy said that. Mark Tansey. That's a quote. I found it just now on the internet.

SAMUEL Good for you.

DARRYL So, do you have any idea how many people will see that picture in my gallery? Okay, most of them won't care, most will be drooling idiots, okay, but the law of averages says every so often somebody will whiz by it and go: "Hey. Nice picture. That Mark Tansey kicks ass." How many people look at it right now, every day?

SAMUEL None.

DARRYL None?

SAMUEL It's in storage at the moment. In the basement of my gallery.

DARRYL You're shitting me. That's horrible. A fantastic picture like that? Nobody sees it?

SAMUEL You don't even know what it looks like.

DARRYL No, sure, but still. You keep it, nobody sees it, you sell it to me, thousands and thousands see it. What we have here is a clear, compelling moral whaddaya-callit. I mean, hey, is it even art if nobody looks at it?

There's a pause.

There we go. I got you thinking. I knew it wasn't going to be money with this guy.

SAMUEL Darryl?

DARRYL Samuel?

SAMUEL I want you to know I was about to leave.

DARRYL But?

SAMUEL But I will stay, and you can continue to try and convince me about the value of having this painting in your gallery. The moral argument is a pretty good one.

DARRYL Thanks. That's the friggin' internet for ya, right there.

SAMUEL But if I'm going to continue to participate in this negotiation, you have to do something for me.

DARRYL Here we go.

SAMUEL You have to fire Martino Kesselback.

DARRYL Who? Oh yeah. Done. He's gone. Gives me the creeps anyway. You want me to have him killed or anything?

SAMUEL No! Jesus. Just fire him.

DARRYL You got it.

DARRYL whips out a cellphone, one with an enormous antenna for overseas calling.

Hamish? Me. Listen. I want you to fire someone for me. Yeah. Right now. Kesselback. Yeah, that guy. No, no, don't kill him. Or, wait. (*to SAMUEL*) Just fire him?

SAMUEL Just fire him!

DARRYL Just fire him. Okay? Okay.

He hangs up.

Done.

SAMUEL Thank you.

DARRYL You bet. So, breakfast tomorrow? We keep talking?

SAMUEL Yes.

DARRYL Tremendous. Okay. I'm gonna do some more research. By the time I'm done, you'll be so morally compelled to sell me the friggin' thing, you'll be beggin' me.

He goes. As he passes URI:

URI Hey. You American, yes?

DARRYL Yeah. Sure.

URI I love youse guys.

DARRYL Where're you from?

URI Ukraine.

DARRYL Oh. Well. Good luck with that.

URI Yeah, okay. I come to America soon.

DARRYL Oh yeah?

URI To die, yes.

COLLEEN has entered, and makes her way to SAMUEL.

DARRYL Oh. Geez. Well, good luck with that.

COLLEEN Hey.

SAMUEL Hello. I was just—

COLLEEN No, wait.

URI I'm getting rich, right here, today.

DARRYL Really.

URI I'm selling something.

SAMUEL No. I'm not the person you're looking for.

DARRYL Oh, yeah? Like what?

URI C'mere.

URI whispers in DARRYL's ear.

COLLEEN Are we being watched?

SAMUEL Look, I don't—

COLLEEN You must stay away from my husband. He's not what he seems.

SAMUEL God.

COLLEEN We must pretend we're lovers.

DARRYL No shit?

URI I am shitting you not.

COLLEEN Come up to my room. Bring the goods.

SAMUEL Oh, for God's—

To URI.

Hey! You! Colostomy.

URI What?

SAMUEL Colostomy. Colostomy.

URI Colostomy?

SAMUEL (*to COLLEEN*) Okay? Talk to him.

COLLEEN Oh! I'm— Oh!

URI Colostomy?

COLLEEN Listen, just forget I said anything, okay?

URI Colostomy, lady?

COLLEEN Yes, just a sec.

URI Oh, not this batch.

COLLEEN (*to SAMUEL*) You'd better forget we spoke.

SAMUEL My pleasure.

URI She's a batch, this one.

DARRYL Okay. Good luck with your thing. And a safe trip back to the Ukraine.

URI Ukraine.

DARRYL That's right.

URI Not the Ukraine. Ukraine.

DARRYL You bet, sport.

DARRYL leaves. COLLEEN crosses to URI.

URI So, okay. You got my money?

COLLEEN Jesus. Shut up.

She turns to SAMUEL.

Um, do you mind? Probably best if you don't hear this.

SAMUEL I'd be thrilled to leave at this point.

URI Ha ha. Out of pool, Canada.

SAMUEL (*as he goes*) Yes. Ha ha.

URI Go get girl. Beautiful night, beautiful place, go get girl.

SAMUEL leaves. He has left the briefcase behind.

Hey! Canada! You forgot your—

COLLEEN Shhhh! Quiet! Let's get this done.

URI So, okay, hello. You smell good again.

COLLEEN Have you got it?

URI I got, I got. You got money?

COLLEEN 200,000 US dollars, as soon as we verify you're selling the right stuff. They gave me one of these…

She pulls out a Geiger counter that looks like a hairbrush.

URI A hairbrush?

COLLEEN No, no, it's a, what do you call…

URI Hairbrush?

COLLEEN No, it's, it's—

URI Hairbrush?

COLLEEN No! It's—

URI Brush for hair?

COLLEEN No.

She passes her Geiger counter over his briefcase; it goes nuts.

URI Oh! One of those!

COLLEEN Yes!

URI Don't need it. I got advanced case of thyroid cancer says this is the stuff.

COLLEEN It gave you cancer?

URI Sure. Like everyone else has handled it in my family since 1986. Starting with my uncle's wife's brother, liquidation man at Chernobyl. First guy on the scene. He knew he was dead as soon as they got near the place. They gave him a napkin over his face, said go put out fire. He stole the stuff, brought it home in a tin box in his pants. Dead a year later. Gave it to my uncle, he dies 1991, then my cousin, then my other cousin, then some guy my cousin knows, then other guys, all dead, then me. So it's good stuff. Blow up anything you need. You Irish?

COLLEEN Yes.

URI Blow up half your crep island. You guys still pissed off at the English guys?

COLLEEN No. I'm not that kind of Irish.

URI There's more than one kind?

COLLEEN Can I have it, please?

URI hesitates.

URI You know what? Not until you tell me who's gonna get my bomb. My family bomb.

COLLEEN Suddenly you're interested in who this gets used on?

URI Suddenly, I give shit, yes. I guess I do. I come here, I look at a beautiful place. Before all was crep. Now I see beauty, and I think I don't want you blowing up what is with beauty. Blow up idiots, blow up scumbags, blow up liar jerks—come to Ukraine, we got plenty—but I don't want this used on no good places.

COLLEEN I'm not going to use it.

URI Of course you are. That's the whole point of this stuff, is to use it.

COLLEEN No, I'm not.

URI Then why for you want it?

COLLEEN I want to keep someone else from getting it.

URI Oho! You playing Keep-Away. From who?

COLLEEN Never mind.

URI No, I mind.

COLLEEN You're stalling! What do you want, more money?

URI Know what you are? You're fiery.

COLLEEN If you try and change this deal now—

URI Fiery and spunky and cute.

COLLEEN I'm warning you.

URI Just tell me. Sweetie.

COLLEEN They said this was going to be simple.

JAMES MacAuley enters, drink in hand. He sees them, and hides behind a tree or a bit of architecture.

URI Okay. Don't tell me. Take off top.

COLLEEN What? No!

URI No deal then. I don't care.

COLLEEN Wait a minute.

URI Off with the top.

COLLEEN You're serious.

URI I need a gesture of good face.

COLLEEN Do you think I'm wearing a wire? Is that it?

URI Okay, yes, that too. Must check for no wire. Top off please.

COLLEEN Jesus. Okay.

COLLEEN takes off her top, faces upstage. Both freeze.

URI That's the stuff.

COLLEEN Okay?

URI I love this place.

COLLEEN Okay?

URI Just a second.

A pause. Slowly, URI sits.

COLLEEN Okay?

URI What is it you do in Ireland? When you're not blowing up stuff?

COLLEEN I'm an interior designer.

URI What's that.

COLLEEN I help people make their homes… pretty.

URI Uh huh. And what is it you do in Ireland? When you're not blowing up stuff?

COLLEEN I'm an—you're not even listening to me, are you?

URI Uh huh. That's interesting.

JAMES, who's trying to see what's happening, falls into the pool. COLLEEN puts her top back on.

Hey!

JAMES rights himself immediately and feigns nonchalance.

JAMES Ah, there you are, darling.

COLLEEN James! We were just, I was just… showing this man my breasts. For absolutely no reason.

JAMES Really.

URI We have deal, you see—

JAMES Really?

COLLEEN No!

JAMES No?

COLLEEN No. We have no deal. What are you talking about? I was just… showing you my breasts.

JAMES Doesn't matter in the least, love. The vacation rules are in play. Have you seen our Canadian friend?

COLLEEN No, I—

URI He went to get girl. Maybe.

JAMES A girl? Are you sure?

URI Maybe not. Hard to say with that one.

JAMES Anyway, thanks for occupying the Missus. Do carry on. My poker game's about to start.

URI Poker game?

JAMES Yes. But you carry on.

URI Is card game, no?

JAMES Yes.

URI You play for money this game?

JAMES I expect so.

URI You got empty seat? I love the card games.

JAMES Oh, no. You just stay here and continue with whatever you were—

URI Plenty of time for that. C'mon. Let me play. I got money. (*to COLLEEN*) You got my money?

COLLEEN I have absolutely no idea what you're talking about, you funny little horrible man.

URI Oh, okay. Gotcha. (*to JAMES*) Hang on a *chimlick.*

He picks up SAMUEL's briefcase, opens it.

Holy Crep. Hey. Canada. You mind I take this to play with cards?

Doing a SAMUEL Kneck impression.

Me? Oh, I don't know. I don't have no opinion about nothing. (*as URI*) You sure, Canada? (*as SAM*) I don't know. I don't care. Shut up, please. (*as URI*) Okay. I'm in. I come play poker.

JAMES (*to COLLEEN*) Are you sure? You saw him first.

COLLEEN Of course. We weren't doing anything at all. Just the, you know, the breasts.

JAMES Okay.

URI Let's go.

JAMES Okay then.

URI Now. Poker. How many cards you get?

The men exit. COLLEEN collapses on a chaise and makes a frustrated noise. SAMUEL runs on, looking for the briefcase. He sees COLLEEN, stops.

COLLEEN He took it.

Blackout.

Scene Three

Dawn. SAMUEL hasn't moved since the end of the scene previous. URI is eating an entire loaf of bread and a wheel of cheese.

SAMUEL You lost it?

URI Who knew he'd be so good? I go in, doing my dumb guy from Ukraine act, you know "Oh, is card game, yes? I play one time in hut at home", you know, whole bit, and they fall for it, think I'm backwards jerk with money to lose. Then they play me as stupid, and I take them down, one after another, beat pants off all of them. Except for Irish guy. He spots me right off, I think. Watches me, waits, he can tell I'm not so dumb, and then he takes everything.

SAMUEL Oh my God.

URI So, sorry.

SAMUEL You lost all of it?

URI Right down to the prindars.

SAMUEL Oh my God. It was thousands of dollars.

URI It's true. I feel like crep about it.

SAMUEL I haven't even made the deal yet. You have to get me that money.

URI Or else?

SAMUEL Or, yes, else.

URI That sounds scary. Okay. I see what I can do.

DARRYL enters, carrying breakfast on a large tray.

DARRYL There he is!

SAMUEL Good morning, Darryl.

DARRYL Samuel. And, uh…

URI Uri.

DARRYL Uri from the Ukraine, that's right.

URI No, just Ukraine.

DARRYL What did I say?

URI The Ukraine.

DARRYL Uh huh.

URI It's Ukraine.

DARRYL (*trying to pronounce "Ukraine" the way URI does*) The U-kraine.

URI No. Ukraine.

DARRYL The Eww-kraine.

URI No.

DARRYL The Eww-krane-noh.

URI No! Just say Ukraine.

DARRYL I'm trying, little buddy. The Ewwww—

URI No! Just Uuuu…

DARRYL Uuuu…

URI Kraine.

DARRYL Kraine. Oh. Ukraine.

URI Yes. Ukraine.

DARRYL The Ukraine. Okay. Thanks for the tip.

Turning to SAMUEL.

Hungry? Have a seat. Beautiful morning. Great day to talk postmodern, whaddayacall, structuralist artwork. I was up all night looking up this Mark Tansey guy. Bun?

SAMUEL Thanks.

DARRYL Here you go. So, he's an intense guy. I got this quote, some guy asks him how he paints or something, you know, like: "why do you paint?" and the answer is like a page long, and I can't understand a friggin' word of it. And I'm like: God, if he paints like he talks, then who cares. But then, you know what?

URI (*who has seated himself with them*) What?

DARRYL Then I saw the painting. This "Innocent Eye Test". I found a picture of it on the internet. And you know what?

URI What?

DARRYL It's friggin' funny. I mean it. It's a funny picture. It's a cow, right? And he's looking at a painting of another cow. These guys in lab coats are showing this cow a picture of another cow. It's hilarious. You never told me it was so funny.

SAMUEL The cow is looking at a painting called "Young Bull" by Paulus Potter.

DARRYL No shit. The picture of the cow the cow is looking at in the picture is like an actual picture? In like art?

SAMUEL Yes.

DARRYL Fantastic. Hilarious.

URI Why are they showing a cow a cow picture?

DARRYL They're sort of measuring the cow's response to, like, art. Right? Is that what they're doing?

SAMUEL Yes. That's right.

DARRYL Hey! I did it! I got the Mark Tansey painting! First one I figured out this whole trip.

COLLEEN enters, URI rises and goes to her.

Like, who's gonna know less about art than a cow, right? So they show the cow the art, to see what the cow thinks about it. But the cow just stands there! That's funny, right?

COLLEEN Now, listen—

URI Good morning. Price just went up.

DARRYL Uh, it's supposed to be funny, right?

COLLEEN What?

URI Price went up. You want the stuff, you have to give me asking price plus.

COLLEEN Plus what?

DARRYL This picture? I'm not making an ass of myself by thinking that, right?

URI Plus you get to cover my losses from poker last night.

DARRYL Am I?

SAMUEL Are you what.

DARRYL You okay this morning?

SAMUEL I'm, I'm okay.

DARRYL You sure? Eat something. Have an egg. I think that's an egg.

COLLEEN How much did you lose?

JAMES enters with the briefcase of money.

URI Ask him. Hey!

JAMES Hello, darling. I was just taking this to the front desk, to have them put it in the safe.

COLLEEN What is it?

JAMES I'm afraid it's rather a lot of your friend's money.

URI Your husband out-stupided me last night.

SAMUEL Darryl, I have to tell you something.

DARRYL Sam, I want to apologize. I never should have come on strong with the money and whatnot.

SAMUEL Well, actually—

URI So, tell him to give me the money back and then we have a deal.

JAMES Give you the money back? Why would I do that?

COLLEEN (*to URI*) Can I talk to you for a sec?

She pulls him downstage.

DARRYL I mean, if I had that painting, I'd hang on to it until I knew that it was going to someone who could appreciate it.

SAMUEL You know—

DARRYL And, so, I feel I'm that guy. I get it, now, I think, or at least I'm starting to. That whole bit with the cash, trying to blow you over by sending all that money on ahead, that was stupid. I see that now.

SAMUEL Well—

URI Hang on a chimlick.

URI retrieves his cheese, then returns to COLLEEN.

DARRYL I embarrassed both of us. I'm sorry. I want to conduct this like grown-ups. So look. Give me the money back and we'll start over. We'll conduct this like the two art-appreciating guys we are. Okay?

SAMUEL Uh, well, Darryl, I think that's a good idea.

DARRYL Good.

SAMUEL Except.

DARRYL Except?

COLLEEN What are you doing?

URI Price is now the price plus you get your husband to give me the money back.

COLLEEN I can't do that.

URI Sure you can. You have to. I kinda stole it.

COLLEEN No, I can't. He doesn't know about me.

SAMUEL Well, Darryl, you see, it's funny…

URI He isn't one of you guys?

COLLEEN No. He's, we think he's some sort of terrorist.

URI Like you.

COLLEEN What?

URI A terrorist like you.

COLLEEN Oh! Right! Like me.

URI You just forgot for a second there that you're a terrorist? Wow.

COLLEEN Uh, ha ha.

URI Ha ha ha. Get money.

COLLEEN crosses to JAMES, and takes him upstage. URI goes to SAMUEL and DARRYL.

SAMUEL The money was a bad idea.

DARRYL I admit that. You don't need to rub it in.

SAMUEL No, it's just that I didn't want to have to look after it from the outset.

DARRYL I know. What can I say. I'm a jerk. Let's just forget about it, can't we? Give me the money and let's forget about it.

SAMUEL I'm just saying, you didn't have to go to all that trouble in the first place. I would have been perfectly happy to sell you the—

DARRYL No, I am, okay? I'm a jerk. I've got a lot of money, and I'm a jerk.

URI Hi boys, how's it going?

SAMUEL Hello.

DARRYL You excuse us, Uri from the Ukraine?

URI No, Ukraine.

DARRYL However you say it. Will you excuse us?

URI Just say Ukraine.

DARRYL Mister, I'm sorry, I'll never learn how to say where you're from, okay? I just, I don't know, I come from a place where people don't have to learn how to pronounce the names of other places! I'm a jerk, okay?

URI Just don't say "the".

DARRYL I can't do that! Okay! I'm a stupid, ignorant jerk. Sam, I beg you, let me start over. Give me the stupid, ignorant money I stupidly gave you and let me convince you I'm worthy of owning this painting. Please.

SAMUEL Uh…

DARRYL I just, I really, really like this painting and I want it and I just WANT IT, okay?

MOUI bounds on, runs to SAMUEL.

MOUI Hey!

SAMUEL Hi.

MOUI Hi! You got rid of Kesselback!

SAMUEL I did?

MOUI Yes, you did. You're wonderful!

She kisses him, a pretty good one. She stares at him strangely afterward.

You lost his money?

SAMUEL I, what? No.

MOUI Whose money? Mr. Plate's money?

DARRYL You what?

MOUI You lost all of his money?

SAMUEL No I didn't.

MOUI Yes you did.

SAMUEL No I didn't.

MOUI Yes you did.

DARRYL You what?

COLLEEN approaches with the briefcase. She's about to hand it to URI.

COLLEEN Here it is. But look. James wants something in return.

URI What.

MOUI Oh, shit. He didn't know. Shit, shit, shit. I'm so sorry.

DARRYL You lost all that cash?

SAMUEL I…

COLLEEN He, um, he's looking for a little companionship.

URI Well, tell him he ever come to Ukraine, I set him up with my sister. She's pretty good.

SAMUEL I—

MOUI No, he didn't.

COLLEEN No. Not that kind of companionship. He's looking for someone, well, more, more male, actually.

URI You're kidding! Your big strapping husband likes the boys?

COLLEEN Only when we're on vacation.

MOUI He sure didn't!

URI Tell him to forget it. I'm not that kind of fella.

COLLEEN No, not you. He likes your friend.

She indicates SAMUEL.

URI Oh. Okay. No problem. We have deal.

COLLEEN hands over the money. URI goes to SAMUEL.

Okay here it is. But look. There's something you have to do in exchange.

SAMUEL (*taking the money*) Fine. Thank you. Fine.

To DARRYL.

Here it is. Please take it.

DARRYL Okay, thanks. Sorry. Sorry about that.

URI Canada, we should have a little talk…

DARRYL No, he and I are gonna have breakfast, then finish this Tansey deal. Hey! Sam! Where are you going?

SAMUEL walks off. A beat, and URI catches JAMES' eye, and nods after SAMUEL, indicating that JAMES should follow. JAMES runs off. Lights to black.

End of Act One.

Act Two

Scene One

Which takes place in SAMUEL's hotel suite. It's large, lavish, and has many of the fantastic architectural characteristics common to stage sets. To wit: there are doors everywhere. From stage left to right, we see a set of double doors leading to a balcony (which overlooks the Act One pool area), the door into the suite from the hotel hallway, the door to the bedroom, a closet door, and finally the door to the bathroom. Much of the bathroom is visible to the audience, and takes up some of the stage right playing area. The bathroom (the part we can see) is suitably luxe, and features a large, glassed-in shower stall with several showerheads.

The central area of the room is sunken, with couches and chairs. There is a bar somewhere—perhaps covered by an opulent hanging tapestry or hidden behind a faux bookshelf.

There is a commotion at the door, and finally, SAMUEL enters. He looks carefully at the lock, which gave him some trouble just now. It's immediately after the events that marked the conclusion of Act One. He's disgusted, and, as one does when disgusted, he removes his pants as soon as he's through the door. He wads them up, and throws them down in disgust. His disgust should now be evident. He goes to the bar, reveals it, and pours himself a drink. He drinks. Before swallowing, he catches sight of a briefcase; prominently, blithely, undeniably sitting on a piece of Tuscan furniture. There follows one of the most elaborate and shameless spit-takes in the history of Canadian theatre.

SAMUEL approaches the briefcase with a mix of fascination and horror. He regards it. He suddenly looks about the suite. Finally, gingerly, he touches the briefcase. It sprays him with white powder, and makes the deafening noise described earlier. He picks up the briefcase. He hits it. He hurls it. He kicks it. Finally, the noise stops.

SAMUEL recovers, and goes into the bathroom. He starts the shower. He crosses to the bedroom.

JAMES enters quietly, and seats himself on a couch. He waits. He sees the briefcase, goes to it, removes a shoe, and waves it over the briefcase. The shoe squeals like a Geiger counter. JAMES resumes the couch. SAMUEL, robed, exits the bedroom, and makes for the bar. He pours himself another drink.

JAMES Hey there.

SAMUEL jumps a mile.

SAMUEL Jesus Christ! What are you— How did you get in here?

JAMES I'm sorry if I startled you. The door was open.

SAMUEL No it wasn't.

A beat.

JAMES Yes it was.

SAMUEL No it wasn't.

JAMES Look. Come here.

SAMUEL Why. No. Why.

JAMES Just come here.

SAMUEL I was going to have a shower.

JAMES I don't want your life story, I just want you to come over here.

SAMUEL does.

Will you sit down?

SAMUEL does.

Thank you.

JAMES approaches SAMUEL.

(*who suddenly and inexplicably has a thick Spanish accent*) You in a lot of trouble, mister.

SAMUEL I… what? What did you say?

JAMES You heard me. You in big trouble, Sam Kneck.

SAMUEL What do you mean? Why are talking like that?

JAMES I'll ask the questions, mister.

A pause. JAMES paces.

Just who are you, Sam Kneck?

SAMUEL Well, I'm—

JAMES Quiet!

JAMES paces.

I can't figure you out. You have the money, You make the buy, he loses the money to me, then he makes me give it back to you. What are you up to, huh?

SAMUEL Look, the money—

JAMES Be quiet!

SAMUEL But— Okay.

JAMES And what are you trying to accomplish with the American? What does he know? How does he fit into all of this?

SAMUEL Darryl Plate? Well, he's—

JAMES Shut up!

SAMUEL But—

JAMES These questions, I'm thinking. They're rhetorical. When I want to ask you something, I'll, I dunno, I'll point at you.

SAMUEL Okay.

JAMES paces.

Do you mind if I ask you a question?

JAMES Look, mister. I'm this close to taking you out of here and locking you up, okay?

SAMUEL Locking me up? What for?

JAMES Yeah, right.

SAMUEL What have I done?

JAMES Oh, I dunno, international terrorism, conspiracy to construct a rogue nuclear device.

SAMUEL A what?

JAMES You heard me. So just sit there.

A pause. JAMES sees SAMUEL's drink.

What is that?

SAMUEL It's whisky. I've been up all night. I was going to have a drink and then go to sleep. But then I got sprayed by—

JAMES Let me see. The drink.

SAMUEL hands JAMES the drink. JAMES smells it. He sighs, then drinks it at one go.

You see? You see what this job has done to me? It's being married to that awful Irish woman.

SAMUEL Are you not Irish?

JAMES No, I— Look, mister, I'll ask the questions. Get me another.

SAMUEL No. Please get out of my hotel room.

JAMES grabs SAMUEL by the lapels and hauls him to his feet.

JAMES There's no time! I have to figure this out! Get me another drink, okay?

SAMUEL gets another drink.

Oh, God, this is killing me. It's so close. It was so close. I can't go back there. I can't. The food, do you know what those people eat? It's not for humans, that food. If only she'd just—

SAMUEL has returned with the drink, and JAMES wheels on him.

WHY DID HE SELL IT TO YOU? GIVE ME THAT!

JAMES downs the drink, slumps into a chair.

How do you connect with my wife?

A beat. JAMES points at SAMUEL.

SAMUEL Oh! Uh, I don't know. I have no connection with your wife.

JAMES Do you know she consorts with Achmed Al Ahmed Meehab?

JAMES points.

SAMUEL No. I don't know who that is.

JAMES That's funny. Are you from a rival group?

JAMES points again. SAMUEL doesn't respond.

You see my finger?

SAMUEL Yes, I do, I just, I don't know how to answer that question. I'm not part of any group. I sell art

JAMES That's what all the intel says. Sam Kneck, from Canada, he sells the paintings. According to them, you're just an innocent Canadian schmuck.

SAMUEL I see.

JAMES But we know better, don't we, huh, Sam Kneck from Canada?

SAMUEL Do we?

JAMES Oh yes.

SAMUEL What am I.

JAMES You are some sort of international criminal.

SAMUEL No, I'm not.

JAMES Yes you are. You have to be.

SAMUEL But I'm not.

JAMES Yes you are.

SAMUEL I'm really not.

JAMES YES YOU ARE, YES YOU ARE, YES YOU ARE! You have to be, okay? Ohhh, God.

JAMES starts to weep.

SAMUEL Um...

JAMES Look away!

SAMUEL Are you—

JAMES Look away, for the love of God.

JAMES weeps. SAMUEL looks away.

SAMUEL Here. Sit down.

JAMES does.

Let me get you another drink.

JAMES No!! No more drink!

SAMUEL Are you sure?

JAMES (*sobbing uncontrollably*) Okay. One more drink.

SAMUEL runs to the bar, refills the glass.

When will it end, God? When will it end?

SAMUEL Take it easy. James: it's gonna be okay.

JAMES No, it won't. And don't call me that.

SAMUEL Why not? Isn't that your name?

SAMUEL returns with the drink.

JAMES My name is Miguel Angel Jimenez. I am with Interpol. And you are under arrest, I think.

SAMUEL Now just, take it easy. Breathe.

JAMES (*taking the drink*) Thank you very much.

SAMUEL You're not Irish?

JAMES I am Spanish. I was recruited by Interpol a long time a go. A lifetime ago. I'm a deep-cover operative, investigating a terrorist cell that operates out of Dublin. It is led by that woman.

SAMUEL You mean your wife?

JAMES bursts into tears again. SAMUEL runs for more scotch.

JAMES Oh, God, don't say it! Don't say it!

SAMUEL Sorry.

JAMES Five years. Five years I have been her acquaintance, then her boyfriend, and finally her husband. Oh, God. The very words make me sick.

SAMUEL So, sorry, you've been undercover all that time? Pretending to be Irish?

JAMES Have you seen what they eat?

SAMUEL Um.

JAMES It's unbelievable. God.

SAMUEL returns with the drink.

Thank you. You know the worst part?

SAMUEL The food?

JAMES No. The food is bad, but it's not the worst part. And the weather is awful, but that's not the worst part. And the people are little and look at you all the time, they stare and stare, with their tiny Irish eyes, but that's not the worst part. The worst part… the worst part is… I don't even like women!

JAMES sobs anew, and clutches SAMUEL.

Can you imagine, to be a homosexual and in this situation? What am I saying? Of course you can!

I agreed because I thought it would take a month or two. I would have to get to know her a little, gain her trust, and then wham, swoop in and bust her. But she was too crafty. She hid her activities from me, and so I had to get closer, and closer and closer, until—oh, God! Shall I tell you?

SAMUEL Well, uh—

JAMES We did it! I was ordered to become intimate with her! And so, we did it! We made the love. Oh, the memory!

SAMUEL You know—

JAMES holds him closer.

JAMES And ever since then, the relentless horribleness! Three times a week! Four times a week! The Irish are insatiable. Did you know that?

SAMUEL Well, actually I didn't—

JAMES I think it's had a profound effect on my identity. Hey. You smell kind of terrible.

JAMES releases SAMUEL. He hauls himself to the bar for another.

I was going mad, but they wouldn't let me stop. I was too far in, you see. I had to stay long enough to catch her. But I never could. I watched, I waited, and still I could not catch her. The years passed, I learned to drink like the Irish, and so now I have this terrible drinking problem. And one night during a vacation in Ibiza I let my guard down and she caught me with a young man. And since then I have to pretend I am liking both the men and women, but men only on vacation. It's absurd! We took six vacations last year. So we decided to put her in touch with this Ukrainian, this man who has the plutonium, and then finally arrest her when she buys it from him. Then I will be free! But she doesn't buy it from him! You appear, and he sells it to you! Why? Why do you want the plutonium?

SAMUEL I don't.

JAMES Sure you do. You paid him.

SAMUEL No, I didn't. He stole that money.

JAMES He what?

SAMUEL I'm here to sell a painting. The money was for the painting. He stole it from me to play poker.

JAMES You shitting me.

SAMUEL No I am not.

JAMES Yes, you are shitting me. There's the plutonium there.

SAMUEL That's plutonium?

JAMES Yes. Look.

He runs over, waves his shoe over the briefcase. It's the wrong shoe, and, muttering, he gets the Geiger shoe. It squeals.

See?

SAMUEL I have no idea how that got in here.

JAMES Really?

SAMUEL I think he was trying to sell it to your wife. But I honestly don't know anything about it.

JAMES So, he hasn't sold the plutonium? So he could still sell it to her? But this is fantastic!

JAMES grabs SAMUEL, kisses him on the mouth.

SAMUEL You know, I'm actually not all that—

JAMES Quiet! I must think!

JAMES heads for the bar.

SAMUEL —Gay.

JAMES pours himself another drink. He downs it.

JAMES Okay. Here's what we gonna do.

SAMUEL We? I was gonna have a shower and—

JAMES You find the Ukrainian, and I'll find my wife, and— No. Better. You find my wife and watch her every move. Then I'll—

SAMUEL Look, Mister…

JAMES Jimenez.

SAMUEL Mister Jimenez—

JAMES But you can call me Miguel.

SAMUEL Okay, Miguel—

JAMES Oh my God! No! Call me James! James MacAuley. (*He switches to Irish.*) Call me James MacAuley, for the love of God.

SAMUEL Okay.

JAMES Whatever you do, don't blow it!

JAMES stumbles.

JAMES (*back to Spanish*) Oh, shit.

SAMUEL Are you okay?

JAMES I am drunk again. Oh, no.

SAMUEL helps JAMES to a chair.

SAMUEL Here we go.

JAMES I curse them. I curse them all. Listen to me. You must find them. Bring them here. Let them complete the transaction here, and I will witness it. Then this will all be over!

SAMUEL I don't really think I should get involved in something like this.

JAMES No. You right. Let's just sit down and get to know each other. You got another robe?

SAMUEL You know what? I think I will help you after all. I'll get them both and bring them here.

JAMES Yes. Good. The mission. You help me, then we celebrate. Hide me. There.

JAMES motions to the closet. SAMUEL brings him to the closet, opens the door, and puts him in.

(*from the closet*) Now, hurry, little man! Hurry!

SAMUEL rushes to the door, struggles with the doorknob, and then opens it. Before it closes, he charges back in, and finds his pants. Suddenly, JAMES lurches out of the closet door, weaves to the bar and grabs the scotch bottle. He sees SAMUEL.

What are you doing here! Go! Go! For the love of God!

SAMUEL drops the pants, and leaves. JAMES lurches back into the closet, and closes the door. A pause. A knock at the door, and then MOUI enters.

MOUI Sam?

Finding no one, she walks through the suite, looking in the bedroom. She begins to prepare the room for SAMUEL's return, by closing drapes, perhaps putting on some music. She disappears into the bedroom, and we see the bedroom lights soften. She returns. She spots the bar, and, heading for it, trips over the briefcase. The powder, the deafening noise. As she struggles with the briefcase to make it shut up, JAMES exits the closet with some velocity. He doesn't recognize her, and so he returns to the closet. MOUI finally makes the noise stop. After a moment, she decides to head to the bathroom. Hearing the shower, she knocks.

Sam? Sam?

She opens the door, and looks around. Finding no one, she shuts the door. Thanks to the accumulated steam in the room (and the bathroom's bizarre architecture) we are not able to see her undress and step into the shower. Nonetheless, she does so. Meanwhile, the door to the suite opens (after some lock and doorknob difficulty) and SAMUEL leads COLLEEN in.

SAMUEL This stupid lock. Sorry. Right this way.

COLLEEN All right.

SAMUEL Please, take a seat.

COLLEEN (*she does*) Is this about my husband?

SAMUEL I, um, no. I don't know. Would you like a drink?

COLLEEN Yes please. Gin and tonic.

SAMUEL Right.

SAMUEL lopes to the bar.

COLLEEN I suppose I owe you an apology for being so forward. I wasn't really after you. I just wanted to keep you away from my husband.

SAMUEL Why?

COLLEEN I thought you were someone else. Someone I wanted. But I was wrong. So you should feel perfectly free to pursue James, if you like. We have a very sophisticated relationship.

SAMUEL You do.

COLLEEN It's wide open when we're on vacation. So, have at it.

SAMUEL Ha ha.

COLLEEN Believe me, it's in my interest to keep him occupied. I have my own fish to fry, as it were. (*accepting the drink*) Thank you.

SAMUEL I see. The reason I asked you here was because I wanted to help you and the Ukrainian make a go of it.

COLLEEN Who?

SAMUEL Colostomy guy?

COLLEEN Oh. Why?

SAMUEL goes to the balcony doors.

SAMUEL He's still poolside, I believe?

COLLEEN Yes. I can't get him alone for five minutes. Now he's having a massage.

SAMUEL Okay.

SAMUEL opens the balcony doors. The sound of flesh working flesh, and URI's voluptuous moans.

Excuse me. Um, excuse me, Mister… Uri. Mister Uri?

URI (*from below*) Ugh. Who that? That you, Canada?

SAMUEL Uh, yes. Listen.

URI Hey! Good! I wanted to tell you. I left something in your room for safekeeping. Don't touch it.

SAMUEL I found it. How did you get in here?

URI Your door wasn't really locked.

SAMUEL Yes it was.

URI Not really.

A beat.

SAMUEL Will you come up to my suite when you're finished there? It's rather important.

URI Important how?

SAMUEL Well, um, colostomy important.

URI But you're not my guy? Yes? The Irish lady is my guy? Ugh.

SAMUEL Yes she is, I suppose, I don't really know anything about it, but if you could just –

URI Hey! Ugh. Have you seen her with her top off?

SAMUEL She, um, she's sitting just over here.

URI Ask her to take off top. She'll do it.

SAMUEL Please, will you just come up here when you're done?

URI You bet.

SAMUEL steps back inside, leaving the doors open. The sounds of URI's massage continue.

SAMUEL Well. He shouldn't be too long.

COLLEEN I still don't understand why you're so eager to help us.

SAMUEL Oh, well, I can't seem to keep my nose out of other people's lives, that's all. (*URI's massage groans are building.*) and I just wanted to ensure that if you two had any business to complete, (*URI's groans crescendo, drowning out SAMUEL.*) that you have the opportunity to do so without interruption (*SAMUEL closes the window.*) Really. Another drink?

COLLEEN I've hardly touched this one. You seem nervous, Mister Kneck.

SAMUEL Do I? That's funny.

He sits with her. A pause.

COLLEEN You know, I used to smell like that. It takes forever to get rid of.

SAMUEL Right. I'm just going to go and have that shower. He'll let himself in. Excuse me.

SAMUEL enters the bathroom, removes his robe, and opens the shower door. MOUI screams. SAMUEL, utterly naked, flees the bathroom.

COLLEEN Everything all right?

SAMUEL (*covering the important bits with a throw pillow or cocktail shaker*) Hmm? Oh. Yes. I just. Caught a whiff of myself. (*approximating MOUI's scream*) Whoo-ee! Excuse me.

SAMUEL returns to the bathroom. MOUI has by now exited the shower, and is wrapped in a towel. During the following, COLLEEN notices the briefcase, retrieves her hairbrush, Geiger-counts the briefcase, considers taking it, decides against that, and resumes her seat.

MOUI Sam. I'm so sorry.

SAMUEL What are you doing here?

MOUI I came in earlier; I was hoping to find you.

SAMUEL Oh.

MOUI I'm sorry. The door wasn't locked.

SAMUEL Um, it wasn't?

MOUI Well, not really.

SAMUEL Not really?

MOUI Not overly locked. No. Hi.

SAMUEL Hi.

MOUI But then I got sprayed. I got this powder all over me, and boy did it smell bad.

She smells him.

SAMUEL It got me, too.

MOUI (*simultaneous with his line*) It got you, too. What is it?

SAMUEL I have no idea. It's some sort of nuclear suitcase.

A pause. They look at each other.

MOUI I took a chance that you might like to, I don't know, have a drink or something.

SAMUEL Yes. Sure. Love to.

MOUI Lovely.

SAMUEL Fantastic.

A pause.

MOUI So… I'll just get dressed.

SAMUEL Oh! Right. Ha ha. Me too. (*as he puts on his robe*) The thing is, it's a little busy out there right at the moment.

MOUI Is it? Am I interrupting?

SAMUEL No.

She looks at him.

MOUI Is there an Irish woman out there?

SAMUEL No.

MOUI Yes there is.

SAMUEL Well, yes, there is, but—

MOUI Oh, I'm sorry.

SAMUEL No, it's just, she doesn't mean anything.

MOUI God, I'm so embarrassed. I'll go.

SAMUEL No. Please. I'm glad you're here. But there's a guy in my closet who's trying to do something kind of important. And I'm helping him. And so, but, it shouldn't take too long, and then they'll all go away, and then I'll get cleaned up, and then I'd be glad to have a drink with you. Okay?

MOUI Can I help you and the Irish woman and the guy in the closet in any way?

SAMUEL I don't know. Could you just stay in here for the moment?

MOUI In here?

SAMUEL Do you mind? Not for long.

MOUI No, I love it in here.

SAMUEL Great. Okay.

They stare briefly. They may kiss. They will kiss. A noise from the hallway stops them. It sounds like someone being thrown against the door.

COLLEEN (*calling to SAMUEL*) Shall I get that?

SAMUEL No! It's okay! (*to MOUI*) This is it. Just a moment.

SAMUEL exits the bathroom, goes to the door. He opens it (again, with some difficulty). URI is in a heap on the floor. He's dressed in a robe, he's oily, and he's laughing his ass off.

URI Hey! Canada! Give a hand!

SAMUEL helps him to his feet.

I never had that before!

SAMUEL What.

URI A massage! It's fantastic!

SAMUEL releases him, and URI crumples to the ground.

Ha ha ha ha! My bones don't work! Is fantastic!

SAMUEL carries URI to the couch.

(*to COLLEEN*) Oh, hello. It's you.

COLLEEN Hello.

URI Take off top.

COLLEEN Now look—

URI I kidding. I kidding. I take off my top.

URI wriggles free from SAMUEL, takes off his robe in one smooth rotational motion, and then is back in SAMUEL's arms again. He's very oily, and in his underpants.

Hey Canada. You smell funny. Did you touch my stuff?

SAMUEL places URI on the couch, and he slides to the floor, giggling. SAMUEL picks him up, puts him back on the couch. A beat where everyone watches him. Nothing. Then, slowly, he slides again to the floor.

Maybe I just stay here. So Canada. What do you want? Make me snappy. I got another massage booked in ten minutes.

SAMUEL I don't want anything. You guys have some business to do. I'll just go and give you some privacy.

URI No! Please! Stay!

SAMUEL No, you guys don't need me. (*shouting at the closet door*) You go ahead and take care of your thing.

URI Hey! Stay! You got to hear this. I got a question.

SAMUEL That's okay!

URI Here's my question: how do you people stand yourselves?

COLLEEN Who.

URI All you people. The West is so beautiful. It has so many things. It has hope. It's not all… hopeless. You know?

COLLEEN It's not all like this. I could show you some hopeless places.

SAMUEL Me too.

URI We go to Ukraine, I show you hopeless. Don't even try to out-hopeless me.

COLLEEN Can we get on with this?

URI You know, I always thought hate was like a big sack with rocks in it, and as you walk along, more crep happens, your hate grows, sack gets bigger. And you never get to set it down, your sack, and it gets bigger and bigger? And soon, all your effort is for this big sack. The sack on your back.

But actually, hate isn't like that. You know what it's like? Hate is like gas build-up. It's like a big build-up of gas, and all the effort is to keep it in. Right? Not to carry it around, to keep it in. It's not that hate is a big, growing part of you, it's that it's actually trying very very hard to leave, you see? And if you can just do that, let it go, it will tear out of you and be gone forever. You see? You will be set free from your hate.

So, listen. I'm talking to you now as a dead guy. A guy whose death is immanent. You're a beautiful woman. What ever you've done, there's no reason why you can't just stop it all now. Give it up. Give up making bombs and hurting people, and just let go all the hate and the terrorist feelings and everything and just fart it all away. Fart it away. Send it all off. You'll feel better, trust me. Okay?

COLLEEN puts her face in her hands, and begins to cry. URI struggles up onto the couch and hugs her.

Is okay. Is ooookay. Fart away, lady.

COLLEEN I don't even know what I'm doing here.

URI Is okay.

COLLEEN I don't even want your stupid plutonium.

URI Good. That's good. Me neither.

COLLEEN I really don't. They made me come here to get it.

URI Who did.

COLLEEN My government. They're trying to catch my husband. They say he's a terrorist.

URI Wait. Your husband is the terrorist? Not you?

COLLEEN No. When you contacted me, I went to the government. They said they'd been watching my husband since before we were married, and that they thought he might be a terrorist. They said you must have contacted me by mistake.

URI But I didn't contact you. You contacted me.

COLLEEN No, you contacted me.

URI No. I would have no idea how to find someone like you. What do I know?

COLLEEN But I had a call from someone, he gave me the secret word, he told me where to meet you.

URI So did I. Huh. That's funny.

JAMES swings out of the closet door. He's plastered. He's waving his finger around.

JAMES (*in the Spanish accent*) That's enough! I've heard enough! Nobody move!

COLLEEN James!

JAMES Nobody move! Colleen MacAuley, formerly Colleen Bristonprivit before you roped me into a marriage from which I may never recover, you are under arrest for violating international law. On your feet!

COLLEEN James! What's going on! Why are you talking like that?

JAMES (*to URI*) On your feet!

URI I'm trying, mister.

URI tries to stand, and flops to the ground.

(*giggling*) Sorry, buddy. Okay, okay.

He tries again, and manages to crawl up COLLEEN. He clutches her and tries to suppress his mirth.

JAMES Okay. Kneck. Come here.

SAMUEL goes to him. JAMES tries to give SAMUEL his finger.

Here. Point this at them. Make sure they don't move.

SAMUEL Um, point what at them?

JAMES This! This!

He looks down.

Oh. Hang on.

JAMES plunges into the closet, flings himself about in there for a few moments, then emerges, holding a gun.

Okay. Nobody move. (*to SAMUEL*) Hold this. Shoot, if they move.

SAMUEL Um…

JAMES Do it!

SAMUEL takes the gun. He holds it like a Canadian.

Okay. I'm coming over there, and I'm taking that plutonium. Don't try anything.

A beat. He takes a step toward COLLEEN and URI, then veers wildly, crashes into something and passes out on the floor.

A beat.

URI Well, that's the Irish for you.

MOUI bursts out of the bathroom.

MOUI Sam? Are you okay?

URI Hey! Canada! Look what you did!

SAMUEL I'm okay.

MOUI What are you doing with that gun?

URI I never believed you had it in you, Canada. You showed me.

SAMUEL Um, he gave it to me.

MOUI Who is that?

COLLEEN My husband.

URI Irish guy.

SAMUEL Actually, he's not Irish. He's Spanish. He's from Interpol, and he's been pretending to be your husband. Well, he was actually your husband, but he was just trying to watch you. He knows you're a terrorist. Sorry. Please don't move.

COLLEEN But I'm not a terrorist.

SAMUEL He says you've been consorting with Achmed somebody.

COLLEEN Achmed? (*thinking*) Achmed Al Ahmed Hameeb?

SAMUEL Yes, I think so.

COLLEEN He sells me area rugs. He has done for 10 years.

URI Sorry, what was his name?

COLLEEN Achmed Al Ahmed Hameeb.

URI Hameeb?

COLLEEN Yes. Achmed Al Ahmed Hameeb. He has a shop in Temple Bar.

URI That's funny.

COLLEEN What?

URI Well, there is a terror guy, but his name is Achmed Al Ahmed Meehab.

SAMUEL Really?

URI He once tried to buy this plutonium from my cousin. But my cousin died before they could finish business. Meehab. Hameeb. That's funny.

MOUI (*to SAMUEL*) She's telling the truth. She buys rugs from the guy. The other guy. The first guy. But that's not all…

COLLEEN (*to SAMUEL*) He's Spanish? James is Spanish?

SAMUEL Yes. Sorry.

MOUI No, he's not.

SAMUEL He works for Interpol.

MOUI No, he doesn't.

SAMUEL What?

MOUI He's American.

SAMUEL No, he's Spanish. He became an alcoholic pretending to be Irish.

MOUI Trust me. That guy's American.

JAMES starts to come around.

His name is… Tim, I think.

JAMES (*in an American accent*) Oh, boy. What's going on. I mean (*in a Spanish accent*) what is happening here, please? I mean (*Struggling to his feet, he sees COLLEEN, and switches to Irish.*) Oh, hello darling. What are you doing here? (*He stands.*)

MOUI Tim?

JAMES Yes? What. Oh crap. Who's Tim?

MOUI Tim… Fennel?

A pause.

JAMES (*using an American accent, in which he will thank God remain through the rest of the evening*) How did you know?

SAMUEL It's her job. She's fantastic.

JAMES (*of the gun*) I'll take that, if you don't mind

SAMUEL Um, just a second. No. I don't think so.

JAMES Oh, come on. Okay, I lied about the Spanish, but that's it. I've been tracking this woman for five years. Really. Five awful years.

COLLEEN Hey!

JAMES Sorry, lady, you're fine, but I prefer a different brand of toothpaste, if you take my meaning.

COLLEEN Sorry?

MOUI He's gay.

To SAMUEL.

He thinks you're cute.

URI He sure does.

JAMES Yes he does.

COLLEEN You mean you don't like women at all?

JAMES Sorry, no.

COLLEEN But we've been married for 3 years.

JAMES (*threatening tears*) Don't remind me. I think it's taken a terrible toll on my identity.

COLLEEN Well. That explains all the vacations.

SAMUEL And do you really work for Interpol?

JAMES Yes.

MOUI No.

JAMES No. Okay, Jesus, who are you?

MOUI I'm clairvoyant.

SAMUEL Who do you work for?

JAMES The CIA. I told you Interpol because let's face it, would you have helped me if I told you I was CIA?

SAMUEL Probably not.

JAMES No, you wouldn't have. Nobody wants to help the CIA. People hate us. I have no idea why. Anyway, there she is, we've got her, and the plutonium, so…

SAMUEL She's not a terrorist.

JAMES She—what? Sure she is.

COLLEEN Hameeb. Hameeb, you moron.

JAMES Sorry?

COLLEEN Achmed Al Ahmed Hameeb. He's the guy I talk to every week. Not Achmed Al Ahmed…

URI Meehab.

COLLEEN Meehab.

JAMES Oh. Really?

COLLEEN Yes. God.

JAMES But I have photos, of the two of you. Secret meetings.

COLLEEN He sells me rugs.

MOUI But that's not all.

COLLEEN Yes it is.

MOUI No it's not.

COLLEEN Yes it is.

MOUI No it's not.

JAMES Wait. Were you… were you having an affair with this guy?

COLLEEN I, yes I was.

To MOUI.

Thanks a lot.

MOUI Oh, shit.

JAMES But. But there are rules. We had rules.

COLLEEN I know.

JAMES Vacations only!

COLLEEN I know. But… come on. You were never the most attentive husband.

JAMES Three times a week! Four times a week!

COLLEEN That's what I'm saying.

JAMES There were rules! You can't break the rules!

SAMUEL Please don't cry.

JAMES I don't believe this. I stuck to the rules!

He runs to the bar, grabs a bottle.

And look! Look what I've become!

He chugs from the bottle.

SAMUEL Listen. James.

MOUI Tim.

SAMUEL Tim. It's okay. It'll be okay.

JAMES Ohhh, God. It's disgusting! You know what? I've destroyed myself! For what! For what!

SAMUEL Really. It's okay. It's over now. You can get help.

JAMES I mean, who am I? Who have I become? I—

He begins to cry. Great heaving sobs.

SAMUEL Tim. Tim. Listen to me. Look at me. You're gonna be okay.

JAMES Nooooo.… The terrorists have won.

SAMUEL No they haven't. Look at me. You're Tim. Tim…

MOUI Fennel.

SAMUEL Tim Fennel, and you're American. You're CIA. You're okay.

JAMES looks at SAMUEL.

JAMES It's okay?

SAMUEL It's gonna be okay. Give me the bottle.

JAMES hands it over. JAMES then lunges at SAMUEL, kisses him.

URI All right Canada! Go for it!

SAMUEL Tim? Tim? Okay, Tim. Settle down.

JAMES Let's get rid of these people.

SAMUEL Tim, no, NO, TIM! NO! I'm not, I like women, okay?

JAMES pulls back, looks at SAMUEL.

JAMES You—what?

SAMUEL I like women. Just calm down.

JAMES No you don't.

SAMUEL I do. I do.

JAMES You didn't half an hour ago. What the hell is going on here?

URI It's hard to tell because he comes from Canada.

JAMES Who are you? Who am I? What are we? I suppose next you're going to tell me this isn't pluto—

JAMES picks up the briefcase, and it goes off. He drops it.

URI No, that's the real stuff.

JAMES flops around, trying to get the dust and stink off of his body. URI picks up the briefcase.

JAMES Hey. Gimme that.

URI No. I don't think so.

JAMES That plutonium was obtained illegally and—

URI I don't want it, but I don't think I want you to have it either.

JAMES Why, because I'm CIA?

URI That's right, buddy.

JAMES You see, that's so unfair.

URI You guys have plenty already.

JAMES continues to be plagued by the powder and stink.

JAMES Look I gotta have something to show for the last five horrible years. Give it to me.

URI Hold it, mister. You come over here and something bad will happen.

JAMES Don't you threaten me, you—

URI I'm telling you, you try to take this and I will kick your ass.

URI, still noodley from the massage, has trouble holding the briefcase up.

JAMES Oh, yeah? Listen. I know nine different ways to kill a guy with a sock, okay? You don't want to mess with me, guy.

URI Come and get me, you drunken Yankee poof!

SAMUEL Okay, hold it!

Everyone freezes.

Just, hold it. Nobody move.

JAMES What are you going to do?

SAMUEL I don't know. I have to think. (*to JAMES*) You. Sit down.

JAMES Listen, sweetie—

SAMUEL Sit down!

JAMES Oh, okay.

JAMES collapses on the floor. A pause.

SAMUEL (*to MOUI*) What do I do?

MOUI You'll think of something. Take your time.

SAMUEL Okay.

A pause.

MOUI By the way, I want to tell you I find the way you've taken charge here to be terribly erotic.

SAMUEL (*turning to her*) Really? Because I really kind of—

URI Focus, Canada, focus.

SAMUEL Sorry. Okay. Let me think…

JAMES Take your time. There are a half a dozen agents on their way here right now.

MOUI No there aren't.

JAMES Jeez, lady! Give me a break!

A pause. There is a knock at the door.

MOUI Should I get that? Sam?

SAMUEL I don't know.

URI Shall we take vote?

Another knock.

SAMUEL Okay, um, would you get that, please?

Before MOUI moves for the door, it bursts open. It's DARRYL. He's dragging a very large painting, covered in brown paper.

DARRYL Sam! Look what I did! Now, don't be mad, okay, because I really felt like I had to do whatever it took to—hey, what are all these people doing here?

SAMUEL Um.

DARRYL Well, whatever. I'm sorry to interrupt, but your door was open, and we've got some business to complete.

SAMUEL What is that.

DARRYL It's the painting. It's the "Innocent Eye Test". It just arrived.

SAMUEL It's the painting?

DARRYL I know a guy, he sort of got into your storage thing in the basement last night. I sort of own your building. Sorry. But I thought if we could actually look at it, then that would be the best way to—

SAMUEL Darryl, I'm kind of in the middle of something here.

DARRYL That's okay. (*to COLLEEN*) Hi. Give me a hand, will you?

COLLEEN helps him tear off the paper. The painting is revealed. It faces upstage. URI drags himself to see it, and MOUI and JAMES have a look, too.

(*He's transfixed by the painting.*) Oh my good God. Oh my— Jesus freakin' Christ. I never, I only ever saw little pictures of this thing.

A moment, where everyone watches DARRYL react to the painting's scale.

DARRYL I got to have this friggin' thing.

COLLEEN Oh. Isn't that clever.

DARRYL It is. But you know what? It's more than clever. It's got layers. The whole painting is about art, about who gets to look at it, who's, you know, qualified, and how you get to be qualified, and—

SAMUEL Darryl, can we do this later?

DARRYL (*strangely and suddenly emotional*) No! Listen to me! Everywhere I go, I'm the idiot, right? I'm the big American jerk who doesn't get anything. I don't know how to talk to people, I don't know what to think or to say or how to sit or whatever. I mean, whose fault is it that the only place on earth I don't feel like an asshole is in Las Vegas? The crudest place on earth? Huh? But here's this picture, and I like it, and the more I look, the more I feel like I get it, and I've never, ever felt that way before. Mark Tansey and I are having a, like a conversation through this painting, and Mark Tansey isn't making me feel like an asshole. Okay?

SAMUEL Okay.

An embarrassed pause.

URI Sell it to him. He loves it.

SAMUEL I know he likes it. I would have sold it to him yesterday, but—

URI He doesn't like it. He loves it.

SAMUEL Sure—

URI He loves it. It feeds him. He loves it. What do you love, Canada? Look at him! He has, with his love of that picture, more right to the world than any of us. He's added to the beautiful world by his love of this object. What have we added? We made this. (*the briefcase*) We made this shit. Look, Canada. Do the right thing.

SAMUEL I'm trying to! I've been trying to sell him this thing for—

DARRYL I give up. You win. I'll give you anything you want, Sam. I—hey, what are you doing with that gun?

SAMUEL Just, shut up, Darryl.

DARRYL (*to the room*) What's he doing with a gun?

JAMES It's mine. I'll take it back, please.

JAMES moves suddenly toward SAMUEL.

MOUI Sam!

COLLEEN Look out!

SAMUEL sees JAMES in time to point the gun directly at him, stopping him in his tracks. A beat.

SAMUEL Okay. Everybody, just, hold it.

General freeze. SAMUEL looks at MOUI, who smiles.

Blackout.

Scene Two

The same. Several hours have passed. In the black, we hear SAMUEL's thoughts:

SAMUEL (*voiceover*) Okay, okay, just think. You have to get the briefcase out of the room, away from that guy. But then what do I do with it? Who do I give it to? Won't the Italian police just hand it over to the CIA? I don't know. I don't know. God. How did I wind up like this? What is my problem? This kind of thing always happens when I go away. Okay, okay. Focus, Sammy, focus.

Lights begin to come up. SAMUEL remains riveted to the spot, gun still in hand. MOUI remains supportive of SAMUEL, but is now perhaps perched on something, perhaps filing her nails. JAMES is slumped on the floor, viciously hung over. URI eats from two room service carts that have appeared. The painting is now turned downstage.

(*voiceover*) Okay. Moui. Can you hear me? It's me, Sam. Sam Kneck. Can you hear me? I need your help.

DARRYL and COLLEEN regard the painting.

DARRYL So, he uses a photocopier sometimes. When he's building one of these things, these pieces of art. And he'll reach right in there and fiddle with the toner, with his hands. He likes to play between the mechanical and the manual, he says.

COLLEEN I see.

SAMUEL (*voiceover*) If you can hear me, just cough, okay? Just once. Moui?

DARRYL He's big on setting up a couple of things in direct contrast to each other. Like an original versus a copy, the real versus the unreal, the clear versus the, you know, obscure—

COLLEEN A cow versus a picture of a cow.

DARRYL Yes! Exactly!

SAMUEL (*voiceover*) Can you hear me? Just lift your head if you can hear me.

DARRYL What did you say your name was?

COLLEEN Colleen.

DARRYL Hi. I'm Darryl.

SAMUEL (*voiceover*) Just, I don't know, look at me or something. Can you do that? Moui? MOUI?

MOUI (*startled from her reverie*) Oh! Sam! I'm sorry. Were you talking to me?

SAMUEL (*looking nervously at JAMES*) Me? No.

MOUII Yes you were. Sorry, Sweetie. What is it. Do you have a plan now?

SAMUEL No, I… never mind.

MOUI Okay.

COLLEEN Oh my God!

DARRYL What.

COLLEEN I'm the cow. Look. I'm the cow. Look how intently they're all watching her, and they're asking her to do something she's totally unqualified to do. That's me, that's my situation here. I'm the cow!

DARRYL I thought I was the cow.

URI (*mouth full*) Canada's the cow.

COLLEEN I love this picture. You're going to put it in your gallery?

DARRYL That's my hope.

COLLEEN I'd love to see it.

DARRYL Would you?

JAMES (*from the floor*) Are you flirting with that guy? That's nice.

COLLEEN Look: you're a spy, you're American, and you're gay. I've got to get on with my life.

JAMES No, fair enough.

To SAMUEL.

So? Any closer to a decision?

MOUI Don't rush him.

URI Yeah. Take your time, Canada.

JAMES Look, I sympathize with your dilemma. I do, it's just that I'm the only one in the room that actually wants the plutonium. She doesn't want it, she doesn't want it, you don't want it, the guy that's got it doesn't even want it.

URI That's true.

SAMUEL But that doesn't mean you should have it.

JAMES Look, who are you to go around telling people whether or not they should have nuclear weapons? That's a little fascist, don't you think?

COLLEEN Are you sure that you want to be making that particular argument, Mister CIA?

JAMES Look, you're moving on with your life, the least you can do is let me—

DARRYL I'll take it.

SAMUEL You'll take it?

DARRYL Sure. I'll take it. What is it again?

URI 500 grams of weapons grade plutonium. From Chernobyl reactor.

DARRYL Oh, yeah. Hey, wasn't Chernobyl like 20 years ago?

URI It keeps.

DARRYL Oh, okay. How much you want for it?

SAMUEL Don't sell it to him.

DARRYL What's the going rate?

SAMUEL Darryl, no.

DARRYL No?

SAMUEL No. Don't.

DARRYL Don't you think I'll handle it responsibly?

SAMUEL I… I don't know. Just, don't do it.

DARRYL But why?

SAMUEL Nobody should have it.

DARRYL Somebody's got to have it. It's not going away.

URI That's the problem with this stuff.

DARRYL And I want it.

SAMUEL No you don't.

DARRYL Sure I do.

JAMES Not so easy being the world's policeman, is it?

SAMUEL (*to DARRYL*) You just want to make the deal. You don't want the plutonium, Darryl.

DARRYL Tell you what. You sell me the painting, and I won't buy the plutonium.

SAMUEL What? That's not fair.

DARRYL I know, I know, it's sort of blackmail. Just because I love art now, doesn't mean I'm a better person. Okay, how about this: You sell me the painting, I'll buy the plutonium from this guy and give it to you. Then you can do whatever you want with it, okay?

SAMUEL I don't want the plutonium.

DARRYL Well, Jesus, what do you want?

URI That's right, Canada. You got to say.

SAMUEL Okay, okay, just—

URI (*During the following, he opens the briefcase, and brings out a lead canister.*) It's just a little can of evil. It's like sand. It's pure, man-made badness in a can. It's the exact opposite of that (*indicates the painting*); of you with top off; of all the beauty available here. We shouldn't have made it, but we did. And now it's here, and it'll live longer than you, longer than me, longer than all of us. It's outlived the people whose fault it was for making it. It just exists now, like all of us, single, going through the world, ready to do what it was made to do. Like all of us. Like you, Canada. What was it you were made to do, Canada?

A pause.

SAMUEL Well, I think, I—

MOUI Oh no.

SAMUEL What.

MOUI What's he doing here?

The door blasts open, and MARTINO Kesselback bursts into the room: tall, with preternaturally black hair and a Wayne Newton mustache. He's armed and his nose is bandaged.

MARTINO Where is he!

MOUI What are you doing here?

MARTINO Shut up, Moui. I'll deal with you in a second.

Sees DARRYL.

Hey! Plate!

DARRYL Yes?

MARTINO charges at him, pointing his gun.

MARTINO Why. Just tell me why. Huh?

DARRYL Sorry, have we met?

MARTINO Yes we've met! It's me, Martino Kesselback.

DARRYL I'll need more than that, big guy.

COLLEEN You're the famous mindreader.

MARTINO That's right.

DARRYL Oh, that guy. Sure. You work for me, don't you?

MARTINO I—what? I did. I DID! You tried to drown me!

DARRYL I did?

MARTINO Yes, you did. A Scottish guy came to my house. He put me in a garbage bag and threw me in the pool!

DARRYL Really? How'd you get out?

MARTINO There was no water in it.

DARRYL Aw, jeez. I said NOT to kill you. Sorry.

MARTINO And all because of some guy named Neck?

DARRYL Who? Oh, right.

Pointing at SAMUEL.

There's the guy you want.

MARTINO (*goes to SAMUEL, but asking MOUI*) Is this the guy? Are you Neck?

SAMUEL has no choice but to point his gun at MARTINO.

SAMUEL Yes. Well, no, my name's, the K isn't sil—

MARTINO You had me killed?

SAMUEL No. I had you fired.

MARTINO That's even worse! Why?

SAMUEL Well. You should have been nicer to her.

MARTINO I am nice! She's the one that— Hey! Looking good, Moui. Nice rack and everything.

MOUI God. You're hopeless.

MARTINO What. You got a nice rack, okay?

Appealing to the room.

Am I right or what?

The next four lines are spoken at more or less the same time:

URI No, you right.

COLLEEN Sure, as racks go, you know…

DARRYL Hey, A—number one, as far as I can tell.

JAMES If you like that sort of thing, I guess.

MARTINO See? So…

URI You should see Irish lady's.

SAMUEL How did you find out about me, anyway?

MOUI He called me, and I told him. Sorry. I thought he knew.

MARTINO I went to find you in Toronto, first. Then I flew here. That Air Canada is disgusting.

The next five lines are spoken more or less at the same time:

SAMUEL I know.

COLLEEN So I've heard, yes.

URI Oh yeah, it sucks.

DARRYL Oh, shit, Air Canada

JAMES Horrible, horrible.

MOUI Air what?

MARTINO When I got to your gallery, they were taking the place apart.

SAMUEL They what?

MARTINO Big sign on the front said the place had gone into receivership.

SAMUEL Oh my God.

DARRYL Oops.

SAMUEL Oops?

DARRYL Yeah. Uh, sorry. I guess I leaned on you a little too hard. I guess I sort of ruined your business.

SAMUEL Oh my God!

DARRYL I just, I really, really wanted to buy this thing.

SAMUEL I WOULD HAVE SOLD IT TO YOU ANYWAY!

DARRYL Really?

SAMUEL YES! OF COURSE!

DARRYL You would have sold it to me in the first place? Before I loved it? That's kind of… crass, don't you think?

SAMUEL Look, just take it, okay? Leave me the money so I can start over.

DARRYL Oh. Uh…

SAMUEL That's what you want, isn't it?

DARRYL Well, yeah, it's just that… as your primary creditor, I kinda already own this now, anyhow.

SAMUEL You what?

DARRYL I know. It's disgusting. I'm disgusting.

SAMUEL makes a strangled, frustrated noise.

MARTINO Unemployed, are you? How does it feel?

SAMUEL reels, repeating the noise. JAMES come up behind him, and grabs him. Using SAMUEL's body, he points SAMUEL's gun around the room.

JAMES Okay! Here's what's gonna happen. Me, the plutonium and this yummy Canadian are walking out of here, and nobody's—

MARTINO has tiptoed to the door and is trying to open it.

MARTINO What's the matter with this stupid thing?

JAMES You. You! (*He means MARTINO, who is frantic with the doorknob now.*) Stop that. Come here.

MARTINO stops, sniffles, and turns to JAMES. He takes a step or two towards him, pauses, makes a high, wet noise, then runs downstage to the balcony doors. Tries to open them. Everyone waits patiently while he puts his gun down and fiddles with the French doors. He manages to finally get them open. He's about to throw himself out the window, but he stops. He runs at MOUI, kisses her hard, then runs to the window, maybe stopping to kiss COLLEEN on the way. He throws himself out. A splash is heard. A beat.

Okay. I don't know who that was, but the rest of you—

URI is opening the lead canister.

Hey! What are you doing?

URI pours the granular contents into a pitcher of water.

URI Making Tang.

JAMES Put that down.

URI is stirring the pitcher of water.

URI You watching, Canada? This is how you do it

And URI drinks the contents of the pitcher.

SAMUEL No! Don't!

URI puts the pitcher down.

URI You see, Canada? End of problem. More or less.

SAMUEL What have you done?

URI I figured out what I wanted, and I did it.

A pause. All eyes on URI.

I love you all, okay? I love this whole thing. The best time of my whole life. I—

He gasps. A pause. He burps.

That's funny.

SAMUEL What.

URI I don't feel nothing. This stuff should have blown up my insides, more or less. But I'm okay. Maybe it was no good. That's funny. All this time—

And URI flops to the floor.

Oh, no. Here we go. It's the stuff for sure. Ow. Crep. So much beauty. So much beauty.

A long pause. Everyone regards the body. JAMES breaks the stillness with a huge sigh. He tosses his weapon on a sofa, takes a bottle or two from the bar, and departs. A pause. SAMUEL makes a tentative move toward URI's body.

COLLEEN You'd better not go near him.

DARRYL Sam. Sam. Look at me. I don't know what just happened here exactly, but we've got to get out of here, okay? We need to go.

SAMUEL Why did he do that?

MOUI crosses to SAMUEL. They embrace miserably. A pause. URI rises, indicates that DARRYL and COLLEEN should be quiet, and then joins the lovers' embrace.

URI Wow. Somebody still stinks.

SAMUEL Hey!

MOUI Hey!

SAMUEL How did you?—

URI goes to the briefcase and hold up two canisters.

URI I always pack a fake. In case I get thirsty.

SAMUEL (*embracing URI*) Thank God!

URI Okay. Okay Canada. Hey. What's a high colonyick?

SAMUEL Well, it's—

URI Whatever it is, mine was supposed to start a half an hour ago. Let's go. Let's all have one! High colonyicks for everyone!

DARRYL Absolutely. I'm buying.

URI That's good, 'cause suddenly I got no monies.

DARRYL That's okay. You can come work for me.

Sam. You too. Come with me to Vegas. Okay? You can run the gallery. Any way you want. We'll gut it and start over, okay? We'll unload all the old crap and devote the whole joint to the works of Mark Tansey. We'll even make people walk. What do you say?

SAMUEL and MOUI are looking at each other.

URI What do you say, Canada?

MOUI Yeah. What do you say, Canada?

A beat.

SAMUEL Canada says, yes!

DARRYL Fantastic!

To COLLEEN.

You should come to.

COLLEEN Are you straight?

DARRYL Relentlessly.

COLLEEN Count me in.

URI is at the door now, and can't open it.

URI What's the matter with this stupid thing?

SAMUEL I don't know. It's been giving me trouble all day.

URI Never mind. Right this way, beautiful Irish lady.

URI takes COLLEEN on his arm to the French doors, opens them.

After you.

He tosses her out the window. Splash.

Now yoy, Americano.

DARRYL You bet.

DARRYL follows. URI prepares to jump.

URI Canada. Someday soon, guys like me are gonna stop paying the debts of guys like you. Okay? But not today. Not today, Canada!

Music. With a flourish, URI dives out the window. Whooping and splashing can be heard from the pool. MOUI and SAMUEL, in this, the moment of privacy we've all waited for since they first clapped eyes on each other, kiss. MOUI must hold her nose to do this, because of SAMUEL's lingering odor. Then they take the plunge.

The End.

For added fun, have the company do the curtain call soaking wet.

Michael Healey

Michael Healey trained as an actor at Toronto's Ryerson Theatre School in the mid-eighties. He began writing for the stage in the early nineties and his first play, a solo one-act called *Kicked*, was produced at the Fringe of Toronto Festival in 1996. He subsequently toured the play across Canada and internationally, and in 1998 it won a Dora Mavor Moore Award as best new play. *The Drawer Boy*, his first full-length play, premiered in Toronto in 1999 and won the Dora Award for best new play, a Chalmers Canadian Playwriting Award, and the Governor General's Literary Award. It has been produced across North America and internationally, and has been translated into German, French and Japanese.

His other plays include *The Road to Hell* (co-authored with Kate Lynch), *Plan B* (which won the Dora in 2002 for best new play) and *Rune Arlidge* (which was nominated for the Governor General's Award in 2004).

Michael continues to work as an actor, and is a writer-in-residence at Toronto's Tarragon Theatre.